EXPLODING ISABEL

ISABEL

BY LISA LOOMER

SOME THOUGHTS ON PRODUCTION

The set will say a lot about tone. For that reason, I would hope that it would be as simple as possible. A cartoonish set will tip the tone. A simpler, more intimate set will ground the comedy and allow the play to get deeper in the second act. I have always wanted to see the play done in a neutral space with just a bunch of different chairs. The important thing to convey is that two people are telling a story about how they made a family.

Music is another key element in conveying tone. One production had a jazz score that worked particularly well.

In terms of direction ... Yes, this is a comedy, with the rhythms of a comedy, but comedy is the means to an end. The play is about a serious subject. "What makes family? How do we decide whom we can love?" It should, very gradually, become more "serious" in the second act. The more "real" the comedy is played in the first act, the smoother the transition will be.

Actors with an ease with comedy and a feel for irony capture these characters best. All of the characters are part of Nick and Miranda's story ... and are seen through their eyes. Although, like most of us, Nick and Miranda feel they come from "crazy" families ... even their families should not be played too broadly. It is especially important that the three birth mothers, no matter how bizarre their circumstances, be played with dignity. They are all in pain over having to give up a child.

—Lisa Loomer

EXPECTING ISABEL received its world premiere at Arena Stage (Molly Smith, Artistic Director; Stephen Richard, Executive Director) in Washington, D.C., opening on October 7, 1998. It was directed by Douglas C. Wager; the set design was by Thomas Lynch; the costume design was by David C. Woolard; the lighting design was by Allan Lee Hughes; the original music was by Joe Romano; the sound design was by Timothy M. Thompson; and the stage manager was Martha Knight. The cast was as follows:

MIRANDA .... Ellen Karas
NICK .... John Ottavino
DOMINIC, GARY, BOB,
EUGENE, NEIL .... Marc Odets
YOLANDA, NURSE, PAULA .... Rondi Reed
LILA, THERAPIST, GROUP LEADER, JUDY ...... Brigid Cleary
SAL, RICHARD, JOHN,
CABBIE, VAL, HARVEY .... Nick Olcott
PAT, ADELE, SOCIAL WORKER, LUPE .... Eilleen Galindo
TINA, TAYLOR, JENNIFER, LISA, ISABEL .... Mary Fortuna

EXPECTING ISABEL received its West Coast premiere at the Mark Taper Forum (Gordon Davidson, Artistic Director/Producer; Charles Dillingham, Managing Director; Robert Egan, Producing Director) in Los Angeles, California, opening on July 23, 2000. It was directed by Douglas C. Wager; the set design was by John Arnone; the costume design was by David C. Woolard; the lighting design was by Howell Brinkley; the original music was by Joe Romano; the sound design was by Jon Gottlieb; the stage manager was David S. Franklin; and the production stage manager was Mary K. Klinger. The cast was as follows:

MIRANDA	Julie White
NICK	Anthony Crivello
DOMINIC, GARY, BOB, EUGENE, ATTORNEY	Marc Odets
YOLANDA, NURSE, PAULA	Jane Galloway
LILA, THERAPIST, GROUP LEADER, JUDY	Brigid Cleary
SAL, RICHARD, JOHN, CABBIE, VAL, MARRIAGE COUNSELOR	Fred Applegate
PAT, ADELE, SOCIAL WORKER, LUPE	Eilleen Galindo
TINA, TAYLOR, HEATHER, LISA, ISABEL	Mary Fortuna

CHARACTERS

MIRANDA — 30s, a wonderer, not a cynic, a woman who questions everything.

NICK — 40, Italian American, an artist and a believer.

LILA — 60s, Miranda's mother, WASP, a bit vague, but means well.

YOLANDA — 60s, Nick's mother, a woman of strong emotions.

SAL — 60s, Nick's father, a man of few words but opinionated.

DOMINIC — 30s, Nick's brother, likes to joke around.

PAT — 20s or 30s, been around the block but optimistic.

Tina — 20s, sensitive and searching.

The same actors, with the exception of the actors playing Nick and Miranda, also play:

PAULA — 40s, lived through the sixties, bitter. (Played by the actress who plays Yolanda.)

GARY — Tina's husband, a jock. (Played by the actor who plays Dominic.)

RICHARD — 40s, a lawyer, Paula's put-upon husband. (Played by the actor who plays Sal.)

DR. JOHN WILDE — An infertility specialist, optimistic, charming, matter of fact. (Played by the actor who plays Sal.)

JUDY — A failed actress turned Adoption Facilitator. (Played by the actress who plays Lila.)

MARRIAGE COUNSELOR — 50s. Been there, done that. Wry. (Played by the actor who plays Sal.)

HEATHER — 18, a regular kid, a cheerleader, eight months pregnant. (Played by the actress who plays Tina.)

LISA — A pregnant exotic dancer, tough, sitting on a shitload of feelings. (Played by the actress who plays Tina.)

LUPE — Puerto Rican, proud, a good mother. (Played by the actress who also plays Pat.)

BOB — Miranda's boss.

6

CABBIE — Russian, 50s.

VAL — Gay, trying to adopt.

EUGENE — Val's partner.

TAYLOR — A business woman trying to adopt.

ISABEL — 18, a nightmare.

THERAPIST, GROUP LEADER, NURSES

A note on casting: All actors should have ease with comedy but the ability and proclivity to keep it real and avoid caricature. Please cast a Latina actress to play Lupe. (She will also play Pat, etc.)

EXPECTING ISABEL

ACT ONE

The stage is bare. The opening music is just finishing as Miranda enters. There's more people than she'd thought there'd be. She feels she should introduce herself ... But where to begin?

MIRANDA. *(Smiles; tentatively.)* I am not a ... "happy" woman. I share this with you because you look like you might understand. I have suffered from unhappiness since childhood. A perfectly happy childhood, my mother has assured me, which I, somehow, failed to enjoy. Of course, we were not poor — we were not starving like the people in China, out of consideration for whom, every night, we cleaned our plates. We had enough money — but not too much, which is vulgar ... I had a favorite stuffed dog ... and when that died ... my parents told me to go out and make friends. It is not cool in childhood to look mysterious and sit alone. Adolescence was better, because everyone was miserable and, for the first time in my life, I felt I fit in. Briefly ... *(Pause.)* I won't bore you with the next twenty years. *(A happier subject.)* My husband is one of those people who says things like, "Wow, did you see the sky tonight? You could see Jupiter!" He's happy when his team wins, and even when his team loses, I suspect he's pretty happy yelling — *(Like her husband.)* "Fucking umpire! He should get his fucking knees broken! Fuck!" One day I made a list of all the things he said he "loved" that day. *(Her husband enters with two chairs, listing some of his favorite things.)*
NICK. Grilled cheese, Rodin, God ... see-through underwear, physics, wine, my parents —
MIRANDA. *(With wonder.)* He loves his parents —
NICK. The East Coast, and coffee.
MIRANDA. He actually said —

NICK. I love these things. What can I tell you? *(He sits down and opens the newspaper.)*

MIRANDA. *(Continues, to audience.)* Couple of years ago, I realized that the century was almost over and I hadn't done much. I'd never been to Prague. I'd never done those Pilates … Most of the people I knew were either in chat rooms or fictional … I was about to turn forty, in just thirty-seven months … When my husband looked up from the sports page and said —

NICK. You know what I'd really love?

MIRANDA. What?

NICK. A child. *(She looks puzzled.)*

MIRANDA. *(To audience.)* What do you say to something like that? *(To Nick.)* Why?

NICK. I was sitting in the park, it just hit me — I'm ready.

MIRANDA. How do you know?

NICK. *(Laughs.)* You just do! C'mon, I've always loved kids, you've always loved kids —

MIRANDA. Sure, but they've always had their own apartments —

NICK. Miranda, don't you want to see a part of you, a part of your parents — live on into the future?

MIRANDA. *(Simply.)* My father was manic-depressive and my mother's an alcoholic —

NICK. Okay, well, how about my family? *(She considers … a little too long.)* Look, how about a sandwich?

MIRANDA. All right … *(He begins to fix sandwiches.)*

NICK. I'm talking about bringing a soul into this world — you want turkey with tomato and onion?

MIRANDA. All right …

NICK. You want cheese?

MIRANDA. I'm not supposed to have cheese —

NICK. So what's the problem?

MIRANDA. No problem. It's just … Well, look, I'm not even going into the obvious considerations like — overpopulation? — but next time you're on the Long Island Expressway, Nick, just remember that whatever soul you bring into this world is going to drive …

NICK. Okay … You want mayo?

MIRANDA. *("Are you crazy?")* No, I don't want mayo!

NICK. Okay. What else? *(He brings her a sandwich. She checks for cheese.)*

MIRANDA. Well, have you seen the local school? P.S.-whatever —

NICK. I pass it every day. It's a beautiful school. A magnet school.

MIRANDA. With high-tension wires all over the playground. Which isn't fenced, by the way —

NICK. Well, that's life, Miranda. Last week, two teenagers got killed pole vaulting for their school team —

MIRANDA. And you know what I said to myself? It's amazing they lived that long. It's a miracle nobody poisoned their Halloween candy. *(Takes a bite.)*

NICK. Have a little faith, baby.

MIRANDA. Look, even if you never let him have a Snicker's bar, or listen to rap lyrics — he's still going to watch horrible violent television — because I have to see the news — there's chemical additives in the school lunches — and even if he does manage to lead a charmed life and make it through high school without getting shot — what if he can't find a job?

NICK. *(Kidding.)* He'll join the Army —

MIRANDA. Great. They send him to some third-world country to rape the natural resources and try out their new chemical toys ... The whole region gets destabilized, causing more religious fanaticism, which leads to more overpopulation — *(Sighs.)* God, I just hope I have Alzheimer's by then so I won't really understand what's going on — *(To audience.)* And you know what he said to that?

NICK. Well ... *(Philosophical.)* Shit happens ... *(He goes to the window and looks out. Day turns to night.)*

MIRANDA. *(To audience.)* And intellectually I knew he was right. But he's also the kind of person who wouldn't put bars on the windows of our ground floor apartment because —

NICK. I'm an artist, I don't want to cage the sky. *(Nick kneels and looks up and out the window. The sky absolutely fills with stars.)* Oh, man, would you look at that? There must be a power failure, the stars are so bright. Look at that, will you? *(She kneels and looks out with him. He puts an arm around her.)* See that star up there? The Outfielder? *(She squints, trying hard to see ...)* That's our kid! *(He kisses her — passionately.)*

MIRANDA. *(In the present.)* I don't know if I was a hundred percent convinced —

NICK. *(In the present.)* Well, you didn't say that —

MIRANDA. *(Continuing, to audience.)* But we made love. *(Nick exits with their plates. Miranda's sitting on the floor. To audience.)* Now, I've never had a favorite sport because I don't have ... *(Thinks.)* pep — but I always liked sex, because, for one thing, the other player is usually more complimentary than adversarial ... and you get to lie down a lot … and stay inside. And now — for the first time, I didn't even have to worry about getting pregnant! *(Pause.)* So when I wasn't pregnant after several months, I went to the doctor's. He recommended a book, *How to Get Pregnant*, and I went to Barnes and Noble and got it — along with a few other books like *Cosmic Questions* and the Hawking book on *Time* so the guy at the counter wouldn't think I was so stupid as to need a book called *How to Get Pregnant*. *(A Clerk enters, hands her some books, smirks, and exits. Nick enters and sits. She hands him the smart books, and reads the baby one.)*

NICK. *(Reading.)* This is amazing. Did you know that time is not only linear but vertical?

MIRANDA. No. Listen, the book says we should cut out a few things.

NICK. No problem.

MIRANDA. *(Reading.)* No coffee …

NICK. No coffee? How about espresso?

MIRANDA. You know, maybe you're not really ready to — *(He takes a cigar from his shirt pocket.)*

NICK. What else?

MIRANDA. No cigarettes, and I assume that means no cigars … *(Nick puts back the cigar.)* No jockey shorts, no hot tubs, no wine —

NICK. No … wine?

MIRANDA. And a cold compress on your scrotum half an hour before sex.

NICK. *(With difficulty.)* Okay, none of this is a problem.

MIRANDA. *(Gets up; businesslike.)* Fine. Let's get started.

NICK. Right now?

MIRANDA. It's the twelfth day of my cycle. You want to lie down? I'm going to be on top —

NICK. *(Digs it.)* Okay — *(He lies down.)*

MIRANDA. Because the book says that's how you maximize your chances of a girl.

NICK. *(Gets up.)* Wait a minute. You want a girl? Because — I mean — I'd love a girl, but I was hoping … Look, why don't you lie down?

MIRANDA. I don't want to lie down now.

NICK. Okay, how many times a month do we do this?

MIRANDA. Days ten, twelve, fourteen, and sixteen.

NICK. So how about we go two times for the boy and twice for the girl?

MIRANDA. What are you — handicapping? *(Shrugs.)* All right

… *(She turns on a light.)*

NICK. What's with the light?

MIRANDA. The book says it's better that way. *(Flops down on the floor.)* Okay, I'm lying down …

NICK. Thank you. *(The lights black out for a moment. When they come up she's in a yoga handstand, her legs against his shoulders.)*

MIRANDA. *(To audience.)* And afterwards I did this to help the sperm find their way home. *(She gets right-side up.)* And when they didn't, I went back to the doctor.

NICK. What did he say?

MIRANDA. He said, "Why don't we just have a look at Nick's sperm?"

NICK. *(Laughs.)* My sperm? I'm Italian!

MIRANDA. Well, he wants to have a look at it anyway.

NICK. *(Incredulous.)* No problem. Fine —

MIRANDA. *(To audience.)* But the next week was Thanksgiving, so …

NICK. Look. Let's just forget about all this for a few days and have a nice Thanksgiving, okay? I'll make a nice turkey with homemade raviolis … I'll roast some chestnuts, we'll have a nice pumpkin pie and a nice — *(Bit pissed.)* wine — and everybody'll have a good time.

MIRANDA. *(Shrugs.)* Fine. *(Their families enter with chairs and a table laid out with Thanksgiving dinner and sit down. Four Italians and a WASP.)*

YOLANDA. Delicious! My son makes the best raviolis in the Bronx.

MIRANDA. Manhattan —

YOLANDA. Well, we come from the Bronx. And he learned to cook in the Bronx. I don't eat in Manhattan, so I wouldn't know.

LILA. *(Tipsy.)* Well, he makes a damn good martini.

NICK. Thanks, Lila. So, Dominic, how come you didn't bring the kids?

YOLANDA. The kids are fine.

SAL. More peppers — ?

DOMINIC. Connie's giving me a pain in the butt about the child support.

PAT. Yeah, she wants him to like pay it —

LILA. How is Connie?

DOMINIC. She's a bloodsucking stroonz.

LILA. *(Pleasantly clueless.)* Oh, good.

SAL. Pass the sausage — ?

DOMINIC. So how's the sculpture biz, Nick?

NICK. Great —

DOMINIC. You workin'?

NICK. Well —

MIRANDA. Well, how do you define "working"? Is it the value of what you do — the satisfaction it brings to you and others … or is it a check?

DOMINIC. *(Beat; perplexed.)* It's a fuckin' check —

PAT. Watch your fuckin' language —

DOMINIC. I'm sorry, Mama.

YOLANDA. That's all right, you're a good boy. *(Kisses Dominic.)* You're both good boys. *(Kisses Nick.)* Everyday I thank the Blessed Virgin for such good sons. *(Pat gets out her cigarettes, dejected.)*

LILA. *(Sotto; to Miranda, curious.)* What does the Virgin have to do with it?

MIRANDA. *(Sotto.)* It's a miracle, Mother, leave it alone.

PAT. Well, I have a little miracle — *(Lights cigarette.)* I'm pregnant!

DOMINIC. *(Laughs.)* That's not a miracle, that's a guy who couldn't find an all-night drugstore!

PAT. Zip it, Dominic.

NICK. That's great, sis!

MIRANDA. *(Trying.)* That's — great, Pat!

LILA. *(To Miranda.)* Doesn't she already have one?

MIRANDA. *(Sotto.)* Two.

LILA. Oh dear. I always felt more than one was vulgar.

MIRANDA. You're using your "out loud voice," Mother.

LILA. *(To Pat.)* Congratulations, dear. Who's the lucky … ah…?

YOLANDA. He's a very nice guy. I'm not saying he's nicer than her husband, but at least he's Catholic.

PAT. He's got two kids of his own, but he don't see them, so he's got plenty of quality time for Brittany and Bree —

LILA. Bree?

MIRANDA. Her daughter, mother. Not the cheese.

SAL. More bread — ?

YOLANDA. *(To Miranda.)* So when are you two gonna get started already?

NICK. Well, as a matter of fact … we're working on it! *(To Miranda.)* Right, honey?

MIRANDA. Well —

YOLANDA. *(Thrilled.)* You hear that Sal?

DOMINIC. *(Chuckles.)* They're "workin'" on it … *(Yolanda gives*

14

Nick a kiss on both cheeks.)

PAT. They're workin', and I get knocked up if I sit funny.

YOLANDA. You kids. You don't know what work is! You know how long I was in labor for yous? *(Points to Nick.)* Eighteen hours. *(Points to Dominic.)* Thirty-seven. *(Points to Pat.)* Forty-two. How 'bout you, Lila?

LILA. Oh, I don't remember. *(Sips martini.)* The service at that hospital was very good.

YOLANDA. Well, me, they had to cut me open. Three times they cut me open! I got an abdomen like a subway map! *(Sal has heard it before and rises fast.)*

SAL. *(Raises glass.)* To Ma!

YOLANDA. *(Not to be stopped.)* And you know what? I would have done it with no anaesthesia! *(Grabs the carving knife.)* They could have cut me open with a —

SAL. To Ma! *(They all rise except for Lila who's too drunk.)*

ALL. Ma!

SAL. Salut —

ALL. Salut — *(Lila's head falls on the table … asleep. No one pays any attention.)*

SAL. Arright, the game's on, let's go. *(The table goes off and the guests start to leave, with their chairs.)*

DOMINIC. Listen, you need any pointers bro —

NICK. *(Laughs.)* Hey — thanks, Dom.

DOMINIC. Forget about it. *(Lila wakes up, sees the others have gone, and leaves too.)*

NICK. *(Without irony.)* Well, that was fun …

MIRANDA. Uh-huh … That's really great about Pat.

NICK. *(Hugs her.)* Hey. Tomorrow I'll check my sperm.

MIRANDA. *(To audience.)* And he did. *(Miranda exits. Nick is alone on stage, waiting at a clinic. He looks very uncomfortable. After a few moments, a nurse comes on played by the actress who played his mother. He reacts to the resemblance.)*

NURSE. We've been doing some renovations, so I'm going to have to ask you to give your sample in the janitorial supply room. *(A young nurse brings on a bucket and mop and places it next to Nick.)*

NICK. No problem … *(The older nurse hands Nick a sterile cup.)*

NURSE. Here you are.

NICK. In … here? How do — ?

NURSE. You look like a smart guy. You'll figure it out. You want a magazine?

15

NICK. Uh — sure. Do you have *Art News*? *(She hands him a* Hustler *and both nurses exit. Nick sits. Looks at the mop and bucket next to him. Moves it just a bit away. The lights fade on Nick, looking lonely. When the lights come up, another man is seated next to him, and we're in a waiting room. This man is played by the actor who plays his brother. They're both holding their little cups. They exchange an awkward look. The young nurse enters, takes the other man's cup, and goes to Nick. Nick offers his cup.)* Uh … here.

YOUNG NURSE. *(Squawks.)* That's it!? *(She leaves, chuckling. The other guy smirks at Nick, macho, hitches up his trousers and leaves. Nick goes to the apartment and starts work on a huge lump of clay. After a moment, Miranda enters.)*

MIRANDA. Hi.

NICK. Hey! Where've you been?

MIRANDA. Work. Oh, and I went to the supermarket to get dinner —

NICK. *(Stunned.)* You went to the A&P?

MIRANDA. *(Pleased with herself.)* Yes I did. And, you know, there was this woman there with this small child — *(A blowsy mom comes on with a full shopping cart and a doll in her arms.)*

NICK. Yeah? How old?

MIRANDA. About five or six. *(The mom tosses the doll offstage. A child pops up from under the junk food in the cart.)* And he was looking around at all the junk they have …

BOY. Wow!

MIRANDA. And his mother kept yelling at him to —

MOM. "Quit touching and sit still!"

MIRANDA. But inevitably he reached out to touch something, I think it was the tiger on a box of those frosted loopy things —

BOY. Frosted Flakes!

MIRANDA. Whatever — and all of a sudden — this great big puffy hand with rhinestone-studded nails landed him one right upside his little head. *(The mom bops the poor kid.)*

BOY. Ow!

NICK. Jesus —

MIRANDA. *(Incredulous.)* And all of a sudden, this — other hand — grabbed the woman's arm, and this other voice yelled — *(Grabs woman's arm.)* DON'T YOU HIT THAT KID LIKE THAT! WHO THE HELL DO YOU THINK YOU ARE?

MOM. I'm his goddamn mother! Who the hell are you?

MIRANDA. *(To Nick.)* And I was … stumped. Because … who

16

am I?

MOM. Whadda you know?

MIRANDA. Well — I know you shouldn't hit a kid!

MOM. 'Cause you never had a kid to drive you crazy enough to wanna hit! You don't even know what box Tony the Tiger's on. You haven't got a clue. *(She exits.)*

NICK. What a bitch. So what'd you do?

MIRANDA. Well, I went up and down the aisles, looking at all this stuff I never even have to think about … *(With wonder.)* Pampers, goldfish food, chewable vitamins … hot dog rolls, grape jelly, double-duty detergent — pink barrettes! … And I thought — that puffy unenlightened woman with the rhinestones in her nails was completely right about me — *(The mom pokes her head in.)*

MOM. You haven't got a clue. *(Miranda takes the newspaper from her bag.)*

MIRANDA. *(Sits.)* Then I stopped for some juice and read the obituaries. Listen to this, Nick. "Kivel, Lillian, beloved mother of Bonnie" … "Chudnow, Harry, cherished pop pop of Kathy Gersh" … "Braiker, Anita, a talented dress designer, she devoted herself to family throughout her long and happy life" — *(Puts paper down.)* What are you going to say about me, Nick?

NICK. Nothing. I'm going to die first.

MIRANDA. Great. Then some stranger will have to say it. "She died and she didn't have a clue." *(Pause; vulnerable.)* But if we had a child …

NICK. *(Excited.)* You're sure now?

MIRANDA. I'm getting pretty sure! *(They hug.)*

NICK. Well, I got my results back from the doctor. You want the good news or the bad?

MIRANDA. Gimme the bad news first.

NICK. He gave me the name of an infertility specialist.

MIRANDA. And the good news?

NICK. Sperm's fine.

MIRANDA. So if I'm fine and you're fine, why — ?

NICK. That's what we're going to the infertility specialist to find out. Oh — and he also gave me the number of a support group —

MIRANDA. I don't want support, I hate support! *(In the present.)* The support group was your idea — *(A support group starts to enter.)*

NICK. *(In the present.)* Let's just tell the story, honey —

MIRANDA. Okay — *(To the support group.)* But there's nothing wrong with us! *(The group doesn't know whether to stay or go. To*

17

audience.) Except that after three more months, we still weren't pregnant — *(The group stays. To Nick.)* So what are a bunch of infertile strangers going to tell us that we don't already know? *(Richard approaches Nick and Miranda.)*

RICHARD. Hi. I'm Richard. I have a varicocele. *(Points.)* In my testicle. *(Paula, Richard's wife, introduces herself.)*

PAULA. *(Bit tough.)* I'm Paula. I only have one tube.

NICK. I beg your — ?

PAULA. I lived through the sixties, I had a good time, you play, you pay, now I only have one tube. *(Tina offers her hand.)*

TINA. Tina. Endometriosis.

NICK. *(Shaking hands.)* Nick. Saraceni. *(Miranda shakes her head indicating, "That wasn't her name." Everyone sits. Gary hasn't said anything. Gary's the macho guy from the clinic — and Tina's husband.)*

TINA. Gary?

GARY. Oh — I'm fine. *(Re: Tina.)* We're married …

TINA. *(Brightly.)* We just started in vitro.

PAULA. *(Not brightly.)* We're doing GIFT — *(The therapist is played by the actress who played Miranda's mother.)*

THERAPIST. And, as I mentioned on the phone, I've done GIFT, ZIFT, and IVF with ICSI … *(Beams.)* And now I'm a mom.

MIRANDA. *(Encouraged.)* So you actually had a baby.

THERAPIST. Triplets! *(Paula glares. Tina bursts into tears.)*

GARY. *(Fed up.)* It's the hormones. She bursts into tears if you just look at her!

TINA. So don't look at me!

GARY. So where am I gonna look!?

THERAPIST. *(Quickly.)* So Nick, Miranda … have you two decided on a doctor?

NICK. Well, our gynecologist recommended Dr. Greene —

PAULA. Greene! Isn't he the one who gave some woman another woman's eggs?

TINA. I think Greene's the one who was using his own sperm!

GARY. Listen, I heard of a woman who saw Greene for IVF and had twins. One was blonde and blue-eyed like Mommy. The other was Chinese. *(Richard and Gary take out their doctors' cards and go to Nick.)*

RICHARD. Let me give you the name of our doctor. He just made the cover of *New York* magazine.

GARY. *(Competetive.)* Well, our doctor's got the best statistics. Here you go. Numero uno. You don't get pregnant in three IVF cycles, the fourth one's free!

PAULA. *(To Richard.)* Give him the card, already!

THERAPIST. *(To Miranda.)* Would you like to share what the problem is, hon?

MIRANDA. We actually don't have a problem —

GARY and RICHARD. Yet. *(The group leaves with their chairs. And Nick and Miranda are waiting in Dr. John Wilde's office.)*

NICK. You know, I heard that people from all over the world come to see this doctor.

MIRANDA. Then he must be very … *(Searches.)* rich. *(A nurse enters.)*

NURSE. Dr. Wilde will be right with you. *(She exits.)*

MIRANDA. So we probably have about an hour — maybe we should see a movie.

NICK. Sssshh, here he comes — *(Dr. John Wilde enters in a white coat and snappy tie. A desk comes on for him.)*

JOHN. Mr. and Mrs. Saraceni? I'm John Wilde. *(Miranda and Nick rise. Miranda shakes John's hand.)*

MIRANDA. *(Nervous.)* I knew that. We have your picture. On the back of your book. *How to Get Pregnant.*

JOHN. *(Warmly.)* Cool! If you like, on the way out, you can pick up a copy of the new one, *So You're Infertile. (He shakes hands with Nick.)* Good to meet you, Mr. Saraceni.

NICK. Doctor.

JOHN. Call me John. I'd like you to think of me as a guide on this journey … a part of your team. *(Nick and Miranda sit. John looks at their chart.)* You're a sculptor?

NICK. Yes I am.

JOHN. I collect a little art myself. *(To Miranda.)* And you work for a greeting card company. Have you written anything I might have received?

MIRANDA. I hope not. I do condolences. I'm working on a new line for pets.

JOHN. Cool! *(No pause; down to business.)* Now, the first thing I'd like to do is to inseminate you with your husband's sperm.

MIRANDA. I think we've tried that —

JOHN. *(Smiles.)* Trust me, I think we can do it better. See, we're going to help nature out a little by weeding out any of Nick's slow swimmers. And then we'll use a catheter to make sure the good guys go the distance. I'd also like to start Miranda on the fertility drug Clomid —

MIRANDA. But I'm not infertile, I — I've been pregnant —

19

JOHN. But since we're not conceiving … the Clomid will help maximize our chances of getting pregnant each time. Now some women experience a few side effects …

NICK. Such as?

JOHN. *(Writing a prescription.)* Oh, bloating … hot flashes … mood swings … nausea … breast tenderness, vaginal dryness, migraine — *(Hands her the prescription.)* But I think you'll do just fine. Any questions, we'll be here. *(Nick and Miranda rise. John leaves with his desk.)*

NICK. Well, he seemed very positive. Why don't I pick up your pills and meet you in the park so we can walk through the playground on our way home?

MIRANDA. Okay! *(They kiss and he leaves.)* For the next couple of weeks, we went to the park almost every day. *(As Nick reenters, the clerk from the bookstore hands him a book.)* We got a book, *Baby Names for the New Century: A Comprehensive, Multicultural Guide to Finding the Perfect Name for Your Baby,* and played around with some names, ruling out the trendy ones like —

NICK. *(Trying it out.)* "Madison" —

MIRANDA. And the ethnic ones like —

NICK. *(Considering it.)* "Quetzacoatl Saraceni"?

MIRANDA. And names like "Faith" and "Hope" which I felt lay too heavy a burden on a child. *(Pause.)* We decided on "Isabel." *(Nick is still reading.)*

NICK. How about "Michaelangelo"?

MIRANDA. *(Inspired.)* Isabel …

NICK. "Leonardo"?

MIRANDA. *(An epiphany; to audience.)* It's "Isabel"! *(Nick exits.)* And, on the day of my first insemination, I woke up at six with a migraine and set about getting a sperm sample from my husband who, not being a morning person, wanted me to dress up a little and help him out. *(Nick reenters against an upright bed.)* So I put on a bustier and some black stockings over my bloated body — *(Miranda goes behind the bed to change and reemerges. A sanitation worker enters, upstage, interested.)* And, unfortunately, the sanitation worker passed by the window of our ground floor apartment at the key moment — distracting Nick — whose sperm missed the sterile cup provided by the clinic … and went shooting across the room. *(The sanitation worker, Nick, and Miranda follow the arc of the sperm with their eyes.)* Being my mother's daughter, I managed to salvage a smidgen of our posterity … *(She bends down and scrapes floor with the sterile cup.)* And I wrapped it in a sock and stuck it in my bustier to keep it warm. *(She does so … and throws on a coat.)* Then I headed out to the clinic because the stuff's only good for an hour and a half. *(Nick exits with the bed.)* By now it was snowing — *(She takes "snow" from her pocket and tosses it over her head.)* And this being New York, I couldn't get a cab. So I stood there in the snow, had a couple of hot flashes — *(She throws open her coat, fanning herself.)* And finally got a gypsy cab. *(A Russian cabbie with a thick accent comes on with two chairs. He throws one of those beaded seat covers over the "front seat" and sits. Miranda sits in back, and they take off. It's the ride from hell.)* Lousy weather, huh?

CABBIE. This is what you call lousy? Maybe you never worked outside digging ditches all day in a labor camp in the gulag.

MIRANDA. As a matter of fact, no …

CABBIE. *(Pounds his chest.)* Fourteen years.

MIRANDA. I'm sorry. Look, do you think we should try Ninth? Because the traffic's not moving —

CABBIE. *(Paranoid.)* So — you are saying I don't know way around city? Listen. After I escaped from prison, I walked across Soviet Union barefoot, with head filled with experimental psychiatric drugs. I think I can find way across town. *(Beat.)* You know what is like to lose your entire family?

MIRANDA. Just my father.

CABBIE. Hmmmph. You have children?

MIRANDA. No. *(Beat; touches cup.)* I don't think so —

CABBIE. Good. It's a terrible world.

MIRANDA. I know. Maybe I better walk —

CABBIE. Please. Do not insult me. *(Rolls down "window.")* Look at that. Picking up after poodle with little shovel and Ziplock bag. *(Yells out "window.")* And children in my country are waiting in orphanages, three in one bed!

MIRANDA. Here, let me give you a twenty —

CABBIE. *(Yells.)* Relax! Read newspaper! *(Throws paper to backseat.)* You see article about teenager who gave birth in bathroom during senior prom?

MIRANDA. I haven't gotten to the paper yet this morning.

CABBIE. She put baby in trash, washed hands, and went back to dance with boyfriend. What kind of world is this!?

MIRANDA. *(Whacks him with newspaper.)* Look. TAKE THE TWENTY AND LET ME OUT OF THE CAB! *(He screeches to a halt. She nearly falls out of the cab.)*

21

CABBIE. Sure. You have nice day too. *(He picks up the chairs and leaves. Honking horns, traffic sounds. Miranda's in the middle of the street.)*

MIRANDA. MOVE! Goddamn car-driving New Yorkers, what's wrong with you? This is a city! Take the goddamn train! COCK-SUCKERS! *(To audience; calmly.)* That was my first month on Clomid. *(A bedraggled streetperson enters. Distraught.)* And while I was waving my arms at the traffic, the little cup was dislodged from my cleavage — *(The streetperson picks up the cup from the gutter, examines it, and hands it back.)*

STREETPERSON. *(Repulsed.)* Here you go —

MIRANDA. Thanks — *(To audience.)* And I stuck it in my purse and ran down into the subway — *(A junkie runs by and grabs her bag.)* Where some junkie stole my purse — !

JUNKIE. Fuck you.

MIRANDA. And my sperm. *(Miranda collapses on the floor. Lila enters with martini glasses and a pitcher, and we are in her apartment.)*

LILA. My poor baby! And you're still not preggers?

MIRANDA. No. *(To audience.)* After three months, I started shooting a stronger fertility drug — *(To Lila.)* And all I got is bloated breasts and a ticket for jumping a turnstyle. *(She goes off-stage to change.)*

LILA. Well, how about a nice drink?

MIRANDA. *(O.S.)* You know I don't drink, Mother.

LILA. Oh, that's right. Who am I thinking of? *(Sips; misses.)* Oh, I missed my mouth. Oh well … *(She pours the extra martini into her glass. Miranda enters, dressed.)* So what are you going to do now?

MIRANDA. Well, John wants to try another procedure.

LILA. *(Surprised.)* And how does Nick feel about John?

MIRANDA. John's our doctor, Mother. He wants to move on to IVF.

LILA. *(Pleasantly vacant.)* Oh good!

MIRANDA. Why?

LILA. I know a lot of people who've done it, Miranda. My God, these days it's practically *de rigeur.*

MIRANDA. Who do you know who's done it?

LILA. Well … *(Thinks.)* Celine Dion …

MIRANDA. You don't know Celine Dion, Mother.

LILA. Don't be fresh, sweetie. You know what I mean. *(Miranda sits on the floor.)*

MIRANDA. Sorry. I guess I'm just a little horrified by the idea of a whole lot of shots and — and procedures — and drugs.

LILA. *(Compassionately.)* Well, you want to be a mother ... might not be bad to get used to a little horror ...

MIRANDA. Right. I don't know why I didn't talk to you about this sooner.

LILA. Well, you come talk to me any time. *(Beat.)* Miranda ... Are you sure you want to have a child?

MIRANDA. *(Worried.)* Why? Are you thinking I wouldn't be a good mother?

LILA. Well, it really doesn't matter what I think.

MIRANDA. I'd like to know what you think.

LILA. *(Laughs.)* Really? Oh dear. You know the last time somebody asked me that?

MIRANDA. No.

LILA. Your father and I were watching the news and he said to me, "Lila, what the hell do you think about this lousy war?" And I said, "You know, Bud, I've never seen anything like it on television." I went in to read you a bedtime story — I believe it was *Eloise* ... And I remember, all night long the television was on. And when I woke up in the morning, all my Valium was gone, and when I went to turn off the TV, he was dead. *(After a beat, Miranda turns to the audience.)*

MIRANDA. All her stories are like that. They have no moral. *(Gets up.)* Okay, maybe a story doesn't have to have a "moral," but if you're going to be a mother, and you're going to tell a story — at least it should ... help.

LILA. *(Sweetly.)* So, dear, whatever you decide ... *(Miranda nods. They kiss and exit in opposite directions. The clerk comes on and hands Miranda some books, and she joins Nick in the park.)*

NICK. You bought more books?

MIRANDA. Children's books.

NICK. Great!

MIRANDA. Your mother ever read you *Eloise*?

NICK. Just *The Agony of St. Teresa* ... What's *Eloise* about?

MIRANDA. It's about this little girl who lives at the Plaza. She orders room service three times a day. And when anything's wrong, her nanny just says, "Fiddle dee dee." It was my favorite book when I was a child. And you know what I just realized?

NICK. What?

MIRANDA. She has no parents. Her parents just left her at the Plaza.

NICK. This is the book you bought for our child?

MIRANDA. The only other book I liked was *Winnie the Pooh*. Same thing. No parents. Just a little boy and a lot of oddball animals. The bear's a compulsive overeater, the kangaroo gets her kid high on cough medecine, the little donkey is clinically depressed, the tiger's got A.D.D. … There's absolutely no adult guidance. No wonder I'm scared shit to be a parent, Nick! Even in fiction, I had no role models!

NICK. Well, don't worry about it. I had role models. *(Gets up.)* *The Brady Bunch, The Partridge Family* — *(He sings a bit of a sitcom theme song.)* Come on, it's time to see John. *(John enters, and they are in his office.)*

JOHN. *(Cheerful.)* Well, Nick, the next thing I'd like to do is have a look at your sperm.

NICK. *(Lightly.)* Oh, our other doctor already looked at it and it's fine.

JOHN. Well, the count's fine, the motility's well within the range of … average … Still, it is possible the sperm's not penetrating the egg at all …

NICK. What?

JOHN. I'd like to do a hamster test just to make sure.

NICK. What?

JOHN. It's perfectly routine. We're just going to put your sperm with the egg of a hamster, and see if the sperm can penetrate the egg. *(He exits. Nick's mother rushes on.)*

YOLANDA. *(Shocked.)* It's a what?

NICK. Nothing to worry about, mom. They're just going to take some of my … *(This isn't easy.)* Okay, see, what they want to do is … *(Tries again.)* Here's the thing. They just want to mix a little of my …

YOLANDA. With the hamster's…?

NICK. Well, that's how —

YOLANDA. You're gonna have sex with the hamster —

MIRANDA. *(Philosophically.)* Well, how do you define sex — ?

YOLANDA. I don't. I don't gotta define it and I don't even got to talk about it because I just did it without making a federal case and nine months later I had a kid. Dear mother of God in heaven. Now I got to skip my haircut and get off the train at Ninety-Sixth and say a novena for you — *(To Miranda; restrained.)* Because I don't know about no Episcopalians — but for us this is a sin! And it's unsanitary. Let me tell you something, if God wanted you to have a kid, you would have had one by now.

MIRANDA. Oh, so what should we do? Get a divorce?

YOLANDA. *(To Nick.)* Can I smack her?

NICK. No. Look, how about a sandwich?

YOLANDA. Make me a ham and cheese.

NICK. *(Jokes.)* Pffft. You're a ham and cheese. *(Beat.)* Sorry — *(He goes off to make a sandwich. Yolanda sits with Miranda.)*

YOLANDA. *(Trying to be helpful.)* Okay, look. Sometimes things turn out good. Sometimes you suffer.

MIRANDA. Why?

YOLANDA. Maybe you did something bad …

MIRANDA. Oh, right, God is punishing me for having an abortion, and he's blessing the crack addict next door with her seventh learning-disabled child. *(Pause. Yolanda rises.)*

YOLANDA. *(Very quietly.)* Abortion … *(Nick enters with a knife and sandwich on a plate.)*

NICK. *(To Miranda.)* You have to do this?

MIRANDA. *(Horrified.)* Sorry! *(To Yolanda.)* Don't worry, it wasn't his.

NICK. So don't have a stroke, Ma, because —

YOLANDA. It wasn't yours.

MIRANDA. It was before we even — *(Suddenly, Yolanda grabs the knife Nick used to make the sandwich.)*

YOLANDA. Give me that. *(She thrusts the knife into the sandwich.)* That's what you're doing to my heart! *(To Miranda.)* You don't cook anything, you don't make dinner — *(Wipes knife, hands it to Miranda.)* Here, why don't you just cut out my heart?

MIRANDA. I'm really sorry. I'm feeling a little out of control. *(Starts to cry.)* I'm taking a lot of drugs —

YOLANDA. *(To Nick.)* And you wonder why she can't give you a child. *(Grabs him, pulls him aside.)* Listen to me. This is a test. You're a good boy, a nice boy, and right now you could do real good and talk to Father De Santo and maybe get an annulment. Or you could do bad and give your mother a stroke. This is a test. You hear me? *(Shakes and smacks him.)* God is testing you!

MIRANDA. *(Adamantly.)* Well, so is the hamster. *(To Nick.)* Right? *(Nick looks at his mother. At his wife.)*

YOLANDA. I'll eat on the train. *(She leaves with the plate.)*

NICK. *(Sighs.)* I'll have the test.

MIRANDA. I'll give you a hand so it'll only be one sin. *(He sits. A lab technician enters, played by the actress who plays her mother. She hands Nick a cup and leaves. Caressing Nick.)* Just pretend we're

25

someplace else and not in a bathroom.

NICK. Like where?

MIRANDA. I don't know, how about San Francisco?

NICK. *(After a beat.)* I don't think so. Too hilly.

MIRANDA. Miami?

NICK. Too ... humid ...

MIRANDA. Okay, well, how about Rome? You love Rome ...

NICK. Miranda — for God's sake, the Pope is in Rome! *(Beat.)* You know what I'd really like to pretend?

MIRANDA. What?

NICK. I just want to pretend I'm home. In bed. With the lights off. Maybe the TV's on ... And I'm on top. Having regular old boring sex with my wife.

MIRANDA. *(Hands him the sterile cup.)* Go for it. *(The lights dim, and when they come up, Nick and Miranda are in John's office.)*

JOHN. Well, I have good news.

NICK. Good!

JOHN. I think we've finally nailed down the problem. Now, as you know, Nick's sperm count was just fine. The motility was ... within the range of average ... But the ability to penetrate the hamster egg, on a scale from one to ten, was ... basically ... zero. So ... *(He pauses, smiles.)*

MIRANDA. So what you're saying ... basically ... is that I've had six rounds of drugs, six inseminations, and the good news is now you know ... *(Incredulous.)* the problem is him!?

JOHN. *(Pats Nick's shoulder.)* Ten years ago, you wouldn't have had a shot in hell of being a father. Today we have an answer. The procedure is called — ICSI. *(Pronounced "icksi.")* We'll inject the sperm straight into the egg, and we'll do it in conjunction with IVF, so your treatment will go like this. First we'll start Miranda on a drug which puts the body into a sort of temporary menopause —

MIRANDA. You're going to put me into menopause when I'm trying to get pregnant?

JOHN. Exactly. This will enable us to have total control over ovulation because only the hormones we give you next will be circulating through your system.

NICK. *(Still stunned.)* You're sure it was ... zero?

JOHN. *(Firm pat on the shoulder.)* Yes. *(To Miranda.)* Now these hormones will cause you to "superovulate," producing a number of eggs. We'll retrieve the eggs and inject them with Nick's sperm —

NICK. Which was ... zero?

26

JOHN. Yes it was. *(To Miranda.)* Then the resultant embryos will be transferred back to the uterus, and hopefully … *(Pause; smiles.)* We will be pregnant. *(Pause.)*

MIRANDA. So. "Basically." You're going to throw me into menopause, shoot me up with drugs, take out my eggs, shoot 'em up with sperm, and shoot 'em back in me — *(Loses it.)* BECAUSE HE COULDN'T KNOCK UP A HAMSTER!?

JOHN. Well, you think it over. *(Notices something in their chart.)* Hmmm. Maybe have a chat with your insurance company. *(Smiles.)* We'll be here. *(He leaves. They turn their chairs, and are alone in their living room. A beat of silence.)*

NICK. I'm so sorry.

MIRANDA. Don't be.

NICK. If there were some way I could take the drugs — and give the blood — and get the eggs sucked out of me …

MIRANDA. *(Simply.)* Well … thanks.

NICK. If I could go through the pregnancy, the nausea, the contractions … If I could get cut open with a —

MIRANDA. Well … thanks. *(A beat of silence.)*

NICK. You want a sandwich or something?

MIRANDA. No.

NICK. You want to divorce me?

MIRANDA. *(After a beat.)* No. *(To audience.)* I loved him dearly —

NICK. *(Under his breath.)* Maybe you should have said so at the time —

MIRANDA. Well, I was pissed off.

NICK. *(Indignant — in the present.)* At me?

MIRANDA. *(Bit pissed off — in the present.)* Well, who could be pissed off at you, Nick? You were so … nice! You probably sat there just heartbroken and said something incredibly vulnerable like —

NICK. *(Back in the story.)* You … You still want to have a child? *(Pause. She looks at him.)*

MIRANDA. After all this!? Do you really think I'm going to go through all this and NOT HAVE A CHILD!?

NICK. *(After a beat.)* Maybe I'll just go for a walk. You mind?

MIRANDA. *(Quietly.)* Go. *(He leaves. To audience.)* The IVF required up to four shots a day, and then there were the trips to the doctor … and I was taking a lot of different hormones, so … I guess you could say it became a source of conflict with my job. *(Her boss enters with a card.)*

BOSS. What kind of condolence card is this? "P.S. Your Dog Is

27

Dead"?

MIRANDA. It's a take-off on "P.S. Your Cat Is Dead."

BOSS. This is a condolence?

MIRANDA. For the person on the go. The guy or gal who's too busy to grieve —

BOSS. Miranda …

MIRANDA. If it doesn't work for you, I'm working on a couple of others — *(Looks at watch.)* But right now, I've got that dentist appointment —

BOSS. You've been to the dentist six times in the past two weeks —

MIRANDA. I've got gum problems, Bob, what can I tell you?

BOSS. You can tell me when I can expect your work to get back on par — *(Beat.)* Or, I'm sorry, Miranda, but we're going to have to let you go.

MIRANDA. *(Edgy, emotional, hormonal.)* See!? That's what's wrong with this business, Bob. We're "sorry," we're "in sympathy," we're "offering our condolences" … we never just tell it like it is. So your dog's dead. Get over it! You don't have to "be sorry," just FIRE ME! FIRE ME, BOB! Just say, "Fuck it, Miranda, you're fired!"

BOSS. *(After a beat; simply.)* Fuck it, Miranda, you're fired. *(He leaves. She turns to the audience.)*

MIRANDA. And that's how hormones can change your life. *(She goes to the apartment. Nick is working on a sculpture.)* Hi.

NICK. How was your day?

MIRANDA. I got fired — *(Hands him mail.)* Here's the mail …

NICK. That's not funny, Miranda.

MIRANDA. No … it's not "ha ha" funny. But it's not tragic either. 'Cause see, now I can concentrate full time on getting pregnant!

NICK. And — and what will we do for money?

MIRANDA. *(Shrugs.)* You'll get a job — *(His hands are full of clay.)*

NICK. A … job? What do you mean a job? You mean like a "job" job?

MIRANDA. Sure! Why not? What would you do if we had a child? *(Nick looks stunned.)*

NICK. Well, I thought … I mean, I just assumed … Gee, I guess I never … Well … okay, I suppose. I — *(Beat.)* You really think we both have to have … jobs?

MIRANDA. *(Simply; no attitude.)* Well, not necessarily at the same time … Sometimes I'll have a job, like for the last ten years … And sometimes you'll have a job like when I'm busy being a science project in order to have our child. *(They stand there looking at each other. The support group comes on and takes seats around them. Paula has a silver metal case with her.)*

THERAPIST. And how did you feel when she said that, Nick?

NICK. Fine.

MIRANDA. *(To audience.)* Ha!

NICK. *(Snaps; to her.)* I felt fine. *(To the group, calmly.)* Marriage is compromise, give and take. I washed the clay off my hands and opened the mail. And I found this letter from our insurance company refusing to pay for the last six months of treatment and denying us benefits for IVF. *(Under his breath.)* 'Cause somebody forgot to get pre-approval.

MIRANDA. *(Ignores him; to group.)* See, their reasoning is that if you have a — a little problem with your sperm —

RICHARD. *(To Nick, hopeful.)* Varicocele?

NICK. *(Emphatically.)* No.

MIRANDA. *(Continuing.)* And you need IVF … You may not be considered a good candidate for IVF because your sperm is bad. *(Beat.)* Sorry. I didn't mean "bad" —

NICK. Yeah, well, you said "bad" —

MIRANDA. But I meant —

THERAPIST. "Challenged." Anybody have any feedback for Nick and Miranda?

TINA. Well, I — *(Gary coughs. She stops.)*

PAULA. Yeah. What are you, like — *(Scrutinizing.)* thirty-seven?

MIRANDA. Thirty-eight!

PAULA. Well, I'm a little older. I lived through the sexual revolution and now I only have one tube. Here's how I see it. I fought for your birth control. I fought for your abortion. You fight for the fucking infertility benefits.

MIRANDA. You know, that's not very supportive.

PAULA. Fuck it. That's how I feel.

TINA. *(To Miranda.)* So what did you do?

MIRANDA. What could we do? We'd been trying for over a year! We put the IVF on Visa.

NICK. Twice.

MIRANDA. But the first two times didn't really count because … *(With difficulty.)* I got cancelled.

TINA. *(Emotional.)* You got cancelled? Why?

MIRANDA. Because the drug they gave me to put me into menopause was a little too effective and … *(With great shame.)* I didn't make any eggs. *(Tina starts to sob. Miranda passes the tissues.)*

29

But we're really hopeful for next time — *(She looks at Nick, hopeful. He's not looking at her. He's not looking at anyone.)*

THERAPIST. *(Moving right along; cheery.)* And how is everybody else doing this week?

TINA. Well — *(Gary coughs, stopping her again.)*

THERAPIST. Paula?

PAULA. Well, the doctor says my body's too jacked up from the fertility drugs to conceive right now, so we decided to freeze my embryos. *(Points to metal case.)* That way if my kid's sterile, she can carry her own sister.

THERAPIST. Anybody else?

TINA. Well — *(Gary coughs. To no avail.)* Has anybody ever heard of santería? *(Silence.)* Well, I have this neighbor who's Cuban and she couldn't get pregnant, and then she did, and she took me to see this woman in Brooklyn who really helped her —

GARY. *(Through his teeth.)* Tell them what you're doing, honey.

TINA. *(Excited.)* Well, I had to buy this honeydew melon in the name of Oshún who's goddess of the river ... And then I wrote a letter asking Oshún for a child, and I put it inside the melon through through this little slit I made on the side, along with six strands of pubic hair from my husband — *(Gary nods.)* Then I wrapped the melon in a yellow handkerchief and lit a white candle to Oshún, and at the end of five days, I'm bringing the melon to the river with twenty-seven cents. *(The group just stares at Tina. Then they get up and leave ... except for Nick and Miranda.)*

MIRANDA. *(To audience.)* And, you know, we tried the IVF with ICSI and that didn't work either ... *(Nick gets up and leaves the stage. Calls after him.)* But I think we should give it another try. *(Silence.)* Nick? *(Nick brings on the sculpture he's working on and starts to remold its head.)*

NICK. How will we pay for it, Miranda? We already owe thirty-nine thousand dollars.

MIRANDA. I know, and I've been thinking about that and I've come up with a plan.

NICK. What kind of plan?

MIRANDA. We'll sell the apartment. *(He just looks at her.)* It's a depressing apartment —

NICK. It's an apartment, Miranda! On the Upper West Side of Manhattan. We own it. The morning light is really good. The maintenance is six-thirty-five!

MIRANDA. Oh come on, do you really "own" anything in this

world? All you really leave behind is your kids — who shouldn't grow up in New York anyway!

NICK. *(Pained.)* Well, what can I say? You bought it, it's really your apartment …

MIRANDA. We'll make enough to pay off our debts, go another round, and then some! *(She kisses him and starts to leave, thrilled.)*

NICK. Where are you going?

MIRANDA. To F.A.O. Schwartz to buy toys! *(She kisses him, and exits. Quick blackout on his reaction. Then she runs on with an armful of stuffed animals. He's not there. To audience; giddy.)* I spent twelve hundred dollars! *(Dr. Wilde's nurse enters in scrubs.)*

NURSE. Mrs. Saraceni?

MIRANDA. *(To audience.)* We went another round! And Nick reached out for support. *(Miranda and the nurse exit. We hear the fanfare "CHARGE!" And Gary and Nick enter … at a ball game in Yankee Stadium.)*

GARY. Nicky!

NICK. Gary —

GARY. Hey, man, glad you called. Glad I had the extra ticket!

NICK. Thanks, man, I really needed to talk. *(They take their seats. Neither says a word. Finally …)*

GARY. So …

NICK. So …

GARY. *(Gravely.)* Tina got her period.

NICK. Oh no!

GARY. Biggest game of the season — Tina gets her period, and Paula takes her to a Bergman festival instead. So how's it going with you?

NICK. I don't know, man. I got to admit … All this … I gotta tell you, I've been feeling pretty —

GARY. *(Cuts him off; yells to umpire.)* Aw — "Strike?" Bullshit! A mile off the plate! *(And then Nick loses it.)*

NICK. Fucking umpire! You should get your fuckin' eyes checked! You should get your fuckin' knees broken! You stupid fuck!

NICK and GARY. *(To umpire.)* Fuck you! *(Miranda rolls on, on a gurney. Her feet are in the stirrups, and the doctor's driving.)*

MIRANDA. *(Like a cheerleader.)* I did my fourth round of IVF — and I made nine eggs! *(We hear the crack of a bat!)*

GARY. *(Re: game.)*	NICK.
Get out, get out, get out —	Go, go, go!

MIRANDA. The retrieval, the ICSI — it all went fine! *(The crowd cheers, as she exits. It's the seventh inning stretch. A man comes on with an adorable little boy and stands right next to Nick.)*

ALL.

    Take me out to the ball game,

    Take me out to the crowd,

    Buy me some peanuts and cracker jacks —

    I don't care if I never come back —

    'Cause it's root root root for the home team —

    If they don't win it's a shame —

(The little boy looks up at Nick and waves. Nick waves back. Nick and Gary start to break down.)

NICK and GARY. *(Singing through tears.)*

    'Cause it's one, two, three strikes you're out …

    At the old ball game.

(Nick and Gary hug fiercely. Gary exits. Nick wipes his eyes, and we are in John's office. John and Miranda enter, and Miranda takes Nick's hand.)

JOHN. I'm so sorry. *(Pause.)* If you'd like to go for a fifth try … *(Pause.)* Well, I can understand your hesitation. *(Beat.)* And there are other courses to try …

MIRANDA. *(Brightening.)* There are?

JOHN. You might want to consider egg donation. Your chances would increase considerably using the eggs of a woman of say, twenty-five … *(Miranda looks at Nick.)*

NICK. Or, how about donor egg *and* donor sperm?

JOHN. Well, if you like …

NICK. And maybe we could get a young surrogate to carry it —

JOHN. If you truly want to optimize your chances, you could do that —

NICK. *("Excited.")* Sure we could! We could get a total stranger to carry the child of two other strangers — who've never even shaken hands with each other, no less with us — or her!

MIRANDA. Nick —

JOHN. *(Nods.)* That would be a "non-genetic but gestational, non-social type mother."

NICK. *("Fascinated.")* Really? What next?

JOHN. *(Enthused.)* Well, right now our team is working on a process in which a child would be conceived in vitro, and development would take place completely outside of the uterus — right up through the time of delivery.

NICK. So pretty soon, you won't really need the uterus at all?

JOHN. Probably not.

NICK. Or — hey, couldn't you just clone her, doc? *(To Miranda.)* You'd have a chance to raise *yourself!*

MIRANDA. *(Stop.)* Nick —

JOHN. Well, if it were possible —

NICK. You'd try it —

JOHN. Of course. *(Pause; sincerely.)* I'm a scientist, Nick. I view infertility as a human disorder, just like any other. Why shouldn't we do whatever we can to correct it? What if you came to me with a heart problem, and I told you a pig's valve could save your life? *(Pause.)* And would I create life if I could? Yes I would. *(He gets up.)* Call me if there's anything else I can do for you. We'll be here.

MIRANDA. *(Rises.)* We'll call you.

JOHN. You take care. *(He leaves. The other actors come on from both directions as a street crowd on Columbus Avenue.)*

MIRANDA. *(Urgently.)* I want to keep trying.

NICK. We're fifty thousand dollars in debt, Miranda.

MIRANDA. I just have a feeling, Nick — I just think we should give it one more try.

NICK. No! It's not supposed to be like this. A child should come from —

MIRANDA. From what? God!? Well — doesn't science come from God?

NICK. A child should come from us! From — love! Look at you. You're bloated — your arms and legs are completely black and blue —

MIRANDA. I don't care! One more try —

NICK. No. We're not doing this any more. Fuck it.

MIRANDA. *(Re: audience.)* Will you watch your language?

NICK. I won't let you do this!

MIRANDA. You're going to tell me what I can do with my body?

NICK. You're like an addict, Miranda! The more you can't have it, the more you want it!

MIRANDA. The only reason we started this whole thing was because of YOU!

NICK. *(To audience; quietly.)* That's what broke my fuckin' heart —

MIRANDA. AND DON'T YELL AT ME IN THE MIDDLE OF COLUMBUS AVENUE!

NICK. IT'S NEW YORK! WHO CARES!?

MIRANDA. I can't stop now Nick.

NICK. Well, I can.

33

MIRANDA. Fine! I'll do it without you! I don't need you to do this! I don't need you at all! *(She walks off the stage.)*
NICK. *(In the present.)* Whoa — get back here! Aren't you going to finish telling the story?
MIRANDA. *(O.S.)* Tell it yourself! *(Nick turns to the audience. Like a deer caught in headlights. Blackout.)*

End of Act One

ACT TWO

Nick is alone on stage.

NICK. *(To audience.)* Okay, I'm gonna pick up the story and help her out. But first, you gotta understand something. I don't like to yell at my wife in the middle of Columbus Avenue — who does that? I was taught to turn the other cheek! Besides, you talked back, some nun'd pull your sideburns. And let me tell you something else. Until I met that hamster — I was a pretty happy guy! *(Glances offstage.)* Unlike some people … Sure I saw some bad things go down when I was a kid — who didn't? I saw Nino Gallata push his brother off a balcony when they were moving furniture. Palmer Di Fonzo — I cut off his eyebrow accidentally with a pen knife — his mother came after me with a gun. Hercules Sorgini, smallest kid on the block, broke his neck in a sled accident, it was like this — *(Leans head on right shoulder.)* For a year they called him, "Ten After Six." And Wee Wee Scomo had a heart attack right on the dance floor in junior high. Doing the Twist. He jumped up, did some splits, never got up again. Best dancer at Holy Savior. What are you gonna do? You gonna tell a kid, "Wee Wee — don't dance"? Besides — *(Glances offstage.)* If his mother had worried about violent television and the crap they put in the school lunches — would it have saved him from the Twist!? *(Yells offstage.)* THAT'S WHY I DON'T WORRY! *(To audience.)* And that's why I've always been a happy guy. Like when I go to the bank. I don't think, "Oh shit — *(A la Miranda.)* "What if the guy on the other side of the cash machine's got a drug problem?" I don't even cup my hand over the keypad when I punch in my pin, which happens to be "Jude" by the way, after the patron saint of lost causes — and not on my worst days — not even on the day my wife left me on Columbus Avenue would I have had a problem telling you that — 'cause, hey, if you wanted to go out later, and use my favorite saint's name to steal my money — *(Yells offstage.)* I JUST WASN'T GONNA WORRY ABOUT IT! Besides … *(Pause; remembers.)* I didn't have any money. I spent my last fifty bucks on paint for the

35

baby's room. And then we sold the apartment. Pretty fast too, because the couple who bought it were expecting a baby any day. Then me and Miranda had that fight in front of this Starbucks they put up where my favorite used art book store used to be … Then she went down to the sperm bank … *(Distraught.)* I did what any guy'd do — *(Pause.)* I went home to my mother. *(His mother enters and kisses him on both cheeks.)*

YOLANDA. I'm so glad. God forgive me, but I never liked her. You want a sandwich?

NICK. Whatever you're making.

YOLANDA. That's what I like to hear! *(She exits. Nick goes to his father who continues to watch TV.)*

NICK. Hi.

SAL. Nick. Good to see ya. What are you doing here?

NICK. *(With difficulty.)* I had a fight with Miranda. *(Pause.)* I couldn't give her a child. *(Pause.)* I can't find a job … I feel so goddamn useless, pop. I don't even know if I believe in God.

SAL. Yeah? *(Beat.)* Go in the kitchen, ask your mother to make you something to eat.

NICK. She's making a sandwich.

SAL. *(Yells.)* Hey, Yolanda — make me one too! *(Yolanda enters with Nick's sandwich. Dominic enters.)*

YOLANDA. Here you go. *(To Sal.)* Yours is coming.

DOMINIC. So where's mine?

YOLANDA. Proscuitto and provolone?

DOMINIC. With a little mustard and mayo?

YOLANDA. You think I don't know that? *(She kisses Dominic and starts to leave. Sal looks up from the TV.)*

SAL. Whoa. Hold on a minute. What do you mean, mayo?

DOMINIC. On the proscuitto and provolone. Wha — ?

SAL. Give him olive oil.

NICK. Pop — !

SAL. Since when do you use mayo?

DOMINIC. I'm dating a girl who likes mayo —

SAL. What you do on the street is your own business. You're not using mayo in this house.

NICK. Pop, he's a grown man —

SAL. *(Explodes.)* I'm not gonna put up with it in my house! In my house you use olive oil! You hear me? *(To Nick.)* And that goes for you too. Maybe that's your problem! Both of yous, sit down, can the chatter, and watch the fight. *(Dominic and Nick do as they're told.)*

36

NICK. *(To audience.)* I stayed for six weeks. But like Einstein would say, time is relative. It's kind of like dog years and people years. Every week you stay with your parents as an adult is equal to about seven years as a child. So I stayed for about forty-two years. *(Misses her.)* And Miranda stayed at Lila's. *(Nick and family exit. Lila enters and we are in her apartment. Miranda enters with a large container of juice and a small grocery bag. She takes a jar of olives from the bag and hands them to Lila.)*

MIRANDA. I picked up some groceries. *(Lila empties the olives into a small bowl and starts fixing a martini.)*

LILA. Oh, thank you dear. How was the sperm bank? Find anyone nice?

MIRANDA. Well, they all sound nice on the forms. But what are they going to say? Six-two, blonde hair, college-educated, serial killer? I've got to think about this. *(Worried.)* You know, they're finding out just about everything's genetic these days — *(Lila is stirring her martini ...)*

LILA. Really?

MIRANDA. *(Nods.)* I read this article in the *New Yorker* —

LILA. Is the *New Yorker* still around? I used to love the *New Yorker*.

MIRANDA. Right. Well, they did this study on twin girls who were adopted at birth. One went to a family in the Bible Belt — conservative, working-class, stay-at-home mom ... And the other went to a liberal, upper-middle-class Jewish family in New York. Thirty years later, the kids meet. Both smoke Kools, both voted for Bush, and they're both wearing the exact same lime green Victoria's Secret pantsuit.

LILA. Lime green? Good God.

MIRANDA. Genetics, mother!

LILA. Well, obviously, the real parents had low IQ's and poor fashion sense! Your situation is entirely different. Your child would have your genes ... and the, uh, serial killer's. *(Sips.)* I wouldn't worry about it, dear. Our genes are very strong.

MIRANDA. *(Looks at martini.)* Right. *(Beat.)* Well, I'm going for a walk. *(She exits. Lila smiles and exits too.)*

NICK. I knew she's show up at the playground eventually. Lila lives just a couple of blocks away. *(Looks at watch.)* And martini time is five. *(Miranda enters the playground and sees him.)*

MIRANDA. *(Tentative; bit cool.)* Hi.

NICK. *(Turns; "surprised.")* Oh, hey — hi. *(Pause.)* How you doin'?

MIRANDA. *(Defensive.)* I'm fine. Well, my hair's falling out, but

they say that's just the hormones leaving my system —
NICK. Looks good. Gives you ... more face.
MIRANDA. *(Smiles despite herself.)* Yeah? How are you?
NICK. Me? Great —
MIRANDA. *(Bit hurt.)* Yeah?
NICK. Well, not "great" ... I'm good ... I'm ... lousy.
MIRANDA. So, uh, what are you doing down here?
NICK. I had a job interview nearby.
MIRANDA. *(Surprised.)* Really? How'd it go?
NICK. Well ... I got it.
MIRANDA. *(Excited for him.)* You did? Nick, that's wonderful!
NICK. Hey, sit down a minute —
MIRANDA. No, that's okay — *(She keeps her distance. He forges on.)*
NICK. I'm painting a mural for a kid's room. Folks live in the Dakota.
MIRANDA. What are you painting?
NICK. Well, the parents are in international law. They want "Guernica." "Guernica" with Disney characters. But they want it in browns and beiges to work with the apartment. *(To audience.)* I knew that would get her —
MIRANDA. Oh Nick. Well, at least you got a job!
NICK. And their neighbor wants me to paint her kid's room too. She wants bunnies on the walls. Bunnies with open arms. Seems her and her husband adopted a child from this orphanage in Romania where the kids spend their first couple of years strapped to a bed. *(Beat.)* And I got to thinking ...
MIRANDA. Yeah?
NICK. All those kids out there ... *(Pause.)* And we're knocking ourselves out to bring another one into the world.
MIRANDA. Who's knocking themselves out? I went to a sperm bank —
NICK. And, you know, I gotta admit I'm just a little surprised you'd do something like that with a stranger. *(To audience.)* This is a woman who's squeamish about taking a lick of somebody else's ice cream!
MIRANDA. Nick, I was just looking into —
NICK. What? Like window shopping? You know, I don't even know if I want to be with a woman who's been with another man's —
MIRANDA. I went to a sperm bank! I didn't make a withdrawal —!
NICK. You didn't? *(She shakes her head no.)* Oh. *(Relieved and moved.)* Well good. That's ... really good. 'Cause you know, I've

been thinking … *(Pause; emotional.)* See, I always thought we'd have a kid with your brains … and my hands. And if it was a girl, she'd have yellow hair … but maybe know her way around the kitchen.

MIRANDA. *(Fighting tears.)* Nick, I — I can't think about that child. I can't talk about that child. I can't. *(In the present.)* Please. Give me a minute.

NICK. Okay. *(She turns away from the audience. Continuing, to audience.)* But last night I'm watching the game with my family and I'm thinkin' — *(Pause.)* What if the kid had my brother's brains and her mother's … *(He mimes drinking.)* I mean it's not like ordering Chinese — *(Miranda turns.)*

MIRANDA. *(Softly.)* We would have had a wonderful child. *(She sits on a park bench.)*

NICK. Yes we would. *(To audience.)* Maybe. *(Sits; to her.)* See, you … and my mother — and Einstein — you want to believe there's some order out there. That if you eat the right lunch — or say the novena — or find the right formula — then things'll work out. Because God doesn't play dice with the universe, right? But what if He does? What if He's got a serious gambling problem? Then what difference does it make if the kid comes from our bodies, or a test tube … or … or if we just adopt? *(Pause.)*

MIRANDA. You want to … adopt?

NICK. *(Looks out at playground/audience.)* Look at those kids. Don't you think you could love one of them? *(She looks out.)*

MIRANDA. *(Trying.)* I guess … I mean — love is love. Right? *(Beat; turns to him.)* You really think you can just love someone for the rest of your life that wasn't related to you at all?

NICK. *(The proof.)* Well, I love you —

MIRANDA. *(Throws her arms around him.)* Oh, Nick, I love you too. I miss you! And I hate living with my mother!

NICK. *(Kissing her.)* Oh baby, I hate living with my mother too! *(To audience.)* So I moved into Lila's because she had a three-bedroom apartment. And now that we weren't trying to make a baby, we started to make love again. *(Lila enters — in her apartment. She sees them kissing and exits fast.)* And we started to talk about adoption. *(Lila returns.)*

LILA. Well, I know lots of people who've adopted.

MIRANDA. Really? Like who?

LILA. Oh … Sharon Stone … In fact, I was just reading an article —

MIRANDA. Really?

LILA. *(Exiting.)* Now where did I put that *TV Guide?* *(Miranda follows her off.)*

NICK. Miranda started to do some research — *(Sal and Dominic enter and sit in front of their TV in the Bronx.)* And I went home to get a blessing from my family.

YOLANDA. Look. You do this, you go away for a year, you come back with a kid — *(Re: Sal.)* and nobody's the wiser.

NICK. No. I want his blessing. *(He shuts off the TV.)* Pop. Miranda and I are thinking of adopting.

SAL. Wha?

NICK. I want to be a father.

SAL. Wha — ? What are you talkin'? It ain't gonna be your kid!

NICK. *(Reasonably.)* Well — what makes it your kid?

SAL. Blood. Blood makes it your kid.

DOMINIC. *(Eating sandwich.)* That's right.

NICK. Maybe not. I mean — what physics is telling us, is that we're all made of the same cosmic stuff. The air you breathe has been breathed in China!

YOLANDA. That's disgusting.

SAL. I don't wanna hear about physics in this house. You see these hands? My father gave me these hands! And I gave 'em to yous! You coulda been Joe DiMaggio with these hands!

NICK. *(Reasonably.)* All right, but I chose to be —

DOMINIC. *(Holds up his own hands.)* Hey, you know my kids have pretty much the same —

SAL. And they're pickpockets!

NICK. *(Reasonable.)* Okay, then why shouldn't I adopt?

SAL. College kid. Maybe if you weren't so busy usin' your *head* — *(Pat enters, pregnant.)*

PAT. Hi! What's goin' on?

DOMINIC. Nick is adopting —

PAT. Great! What's everybody eatin'? *(She eats the rest of Dominic's sandwich.)*

DOMINIC. So what kind of kid are we talkin' here?

NICK. *(Excited.)* It doesn't matter! What physics is telling us is we're all one!

YOLANDA. He'll talk to Father De Santo.

PAT. I know a girl got pregnant, went to Father De Santo — she was in my class at Holy Savior —

YOLANDA. *(To Sal.)* An Italian girl, Sal … who's gotta know?

NICK. Oh for Christ's —

PAT. *(Simply informational, to Yolanda.)* Well, the father was black

— *(Sal and Yolanda cannot find words.)* Maybe black Puerto Rican, I don't remember. *(Sal's eyes bulge.)* But the kid could pass for Italian. *(Beat.)* Well, Sicilian …

NICK. *(To audience; embarrassed.)* I'm sorry about this — *(To Sal and Yolanda.)* Didn't Jesus say, "Love thy neighbor?"

SAL. Jesus said, "Love thy neighbor" — not "adopt him!"

NICK. *(Calls offstage.)* Miranda! *(To family.)* Please — *(He motions for them to leave. They start to.)*

DOMINIC. *(To audience.)* We're not really like this. Only in *his* fuckin' story —

YOLANDA. *(Exiting.)* We're not prejudiced — *(The family exits, and Miranda enters with an armful of books.)*

MIRANDA. Hey! I found some books!

NICK. Good. You know, sometimes I don't even know if I like my genes. I mean, I love my genes, but —

MIRANDA. I know. And guess who I ran into in the adoption section? Paula! From the support group? With one tube? Richard left her for a fertile woman, and now she's joined an adoption support group, and she gave me their card.

NICK. *(Leery.)* You really think we need support? *(The adoption support group enters with chairs and starts forming a circle.)*

MIRANDA. It's mostly about sharing information. I just want to go about this rationally this time.

NICK. Good thinking. Right. *(He kisses her, and they take seats.)*

LEADER. *(To group.)* So why don't we just go around the circle and everybody can tell our new faces what kind of adoption they're involved in? *(The group consists of a gay couple, Eugene and Val, Taylor, a CPA, and Paula. The leader is multiethnically dressed. Everyone is incredibly positive about the kind of adoption they're going for.)*

EUGENE. I'm Eugene … Val and I are hoping to do a private adoption.

MIRANDA. Uh-huh … *(Nick nods.)*

TAYLOR. I'm Taylor, my husband couldn't come tonight because — *(Thinks; gives up.)* He didn't want to … And we've decided to adopt through the state.

LEADER. And you already know Paula?

PAULA. Well, I'm going to China because I want a baby — and the state of New York doesn't want to know from a single female taxpayer over forty-five.

TAYLOR. But you two could get on the waiting list for an infant or even a newborn! *(Miranda nods, rational. Nick's getting excited.)*

41

NICK. Great! How long's the waiting list?

PAULA. For a white kid? Five years to life. *(Nick and Miranda nod, following the information like a ping-pong game.)*

LEADER. *(Encouraging.)* But the waiting list for an African-American or Latino child is much shorter!

TAYLOR. *(Brightly.)* Or a child who's differently abled —

VAL. *(The best option.)* Or an older African-American or Latino child who's differently abled — !

EUGENE. Down's Syndrome is very popular. They're so loving —

PAULA. Yeah, well, I'm going to China. I don't give a flying fuck what color the kid is, I just want an infant so I can have some impact. *(To Miranda.)* See, after three, it's over. Kid's cooked. You got Mother Theresa or Ted Kasinsky. You want to adopt before you hit menopause? Go to China. See, in China, people are only allowed to have one child. And if it's a girl, a lot of people go "Feh" and leave it on the side of the road. So they can try again for a boy child. And boys are just men with smaller … brains.

LEADER. *(Quickly.)* Thanks, Paula. Any questions? *(Nick and Miranda look at each other.)*

MIRANDA. Not really —

NICK. No, I guess that just about —

VAL. Hold on a sec, I had a question. *(To Paula.)* Do they really go "feh" in China?

PAULA. I was simply making the point, for our new faces, that I've been around the adoption block a few times, and nobody wants to know from a single woman over forty-five. ·

EUGENE. *("Surprised.")* And you know, Paula, everywhere we go, people say, "Golly — wish I had two dads myself!"

PAULA. Well, at least you both have husbands. And Val has a child —

EUGENE. Whom he rarely gets to see —

VAL. *(To Nick and Miranda.)* Her mother took her to New Mexico. Don't get me started. It's all very Georgia O'Keefe. *(Nick nods.)*

EUGENE. Her mother's lover refers to Val as "the sperm."

VAL. I call to talk to my daughter, she goes, "The sperm's on the phone!"

TAYLOR. At least you have a daughter.

PAULA. Yeah!

LEADER. *(Jumps in fast.)* Okay, I think we've been around the circle now, so what kind of adoption were you two thinking of?

MIRANDA. *(Unsure.)* Well —

NICK. Gee — *(Everyone whips out cards or writes down names.)*

EUGENE. Listen, let me give you the name of our adoption lawyer —

LEADER. Or, you might want to call an adoption facilitator —

TAYLOR. Or a social worker — *(Everyone gives them cards.)*

PAULA. Or China. *(The group exits.)*

NICK. *(To audience; reading a card.)* But we went with an adoption facilitator named Judy Beech at the Adoption Option — *(Their phone rings.)* Because she was the first to return our call. *(To Miranda.)* Okay?

MIRANDA. *(Remaining positive.)* Uh — okay.

JUDY'S VOICE ON PHONE. *(Warm as toast.)* Kids. I know what you're going through! And the one thing I can promise is, I will find you a baby! *(Judy enters. The most enthusiastic person in the world.)*

JUDY. I will find you a baby!

MIRANDA. *(Thrilled.)* You will?

NICK. *(To audience.)* It was like finding out we were pregnant!

JUDY. And to tell you the truth, I don't consider this a job. It's a privilege! *(Sits.)* See, before this I was an actress, and … *(Bitter.)* Well, let's just say this is a much more fulfilling thing to do. Even if I *had* gotten work … I'm sure that all the money — and the fame — and the travel … *(Jumps up, goes to them.)* Well, I just know that all the standing ovations in the world could never have touched the joy I feel placing a baby in an infertile couple's arms.

MIRANDA. And you've adopted yourself?

JUDY. Well, no. My personal decision has been to be childfree. My work is my way of being a mom. Also I've recently discovered that I don't really like children. But that's just me. Are you familiar with open adoption?

NICK. That means everybody gets to know everybody, right?

JUDY. Right! Say a pregnant woman sees my ad in the Yellow Pages and calls me about placing her baby. I'll send her pictures and resumes of my clients, and she'll choose the couple she wants for her child. So you get to form a special bond with the birth mother. She gets to feel appreciated, supported — *(Sits; mutters.)* Not like some piece of meat in a cattle call that gets tossed out after she sings her sixteen bars …

MIRANDA. And what are these women like?

JUDY. *(Bit defensive.)* They're great! You'll see. You'll meet the right birth mom and you'll just know. "This is right." *(Beat.)* Of course, some are on drugs. Then again, sometimes the mom is totally clean. And Dad's a junkie ... But a lot of our moms are on Medicaid so they've had medical care throughout the pregnancy. *(A plus.)* And some are in jail so you can be sure they've had medical care. And good nutrition.

MIRANDA. *(Dazed.)* Oh — good.

NICK. How about the fathers?

JUDY. Well, it's not too often that you get to meet the dads. They're in gangs, or jail, or they want to be free to do what they want — hijack cars, get high, do regional theatre — *(Quickly.)* But you will get to know the mom! In fact, I had two calls from new birth moms this morning —

NICK. *(Jumps at it.)* How much does it cost?

JUDY. Oh, an adoption lawyer will draw up an agreement about expenses during the pregnancy — say, rent for the birth mother, food for her and any other children she might have ... utilities, phone, car fare ... She might need a stove or fridge, or have immediate debts that need to be taken care of ... Hospital expenses ... Say, oh, two to twenty thousand dollars.

NICK. But — that's it?

JUDY. Well, the lawyer's fee's about seven thousand —

NICK. But that's —

JUDY. And so is mine!

NICK. Fine. *(Nick takes out his new checkbook. Miranda looks surprised.)*

MIRANDA. *(Sotto.)* Really?

NICK. Don't worry, "Guernica" is paying for it. *(Nick hands Judy a check.)*

JUDY. Nick, Miranda ... welcome to the Adoption Option! *(She hugs them and leaves.)*

NICK. *(To audience; excited.)* Judy called the following week.

JUDY'S VOICE ON PHONE. Kids? It's Judy! I just met a wonderful birth mom! Her name is Heather. She's seventeen, she's in her seventh month. So get me those resumes — and pictures, kids! *(Miranda stands and poses. A picture is snapped.)*

NICK. *(To audience.)* And two days later, we had lunch near Heather's house in Jersey. *(Heather enters. Long hair, fresh-faced, a child great with child.)* Heather?

HEATHER. How'd you know? *(Miranda looks at Nick.)*

NICK. Judy told us a little about you —

HEATHER. Oh. *(A waiter sets up a table and chairs. They sit. It's awkward.)*

NICK and MIRANDA. *(Smile.)* So …

MIRANDA. How are you feeling, Heather?

HEATHER. Me? Okay —

NICK. A little tired?

HEATHER. Uh-huh. On account of like work and all —

MIRANDA. Where do you work?

HEATHER. At the Pizza Hut over in Paramus. I'm trying to save up for my prom.

NICK. Well, that's great. I loved my prom. *(Elbows Miranda.)* Didn't you?

MIRANDA. I didn't go. *(To Heather.)* I mean — we didn't have one —

HEATHER. Oh. Are you from America? *(Miranda looks puzzled.)* My friend Liz's mom is from someplace that didn't have a prom. I think it was like Bosnia —

NICK. Well, I had a prom. And it was great. So tell us about yourself, Heather. What do you like to do?

HEATHER. Well, I was on the tall flag team at school. We placed first in the regional championships.

NICK. You must have a great team!

HEATHER. Yeah. But then I had to drop out before the nationals 'cause I got like … pregnant.

MIRANDA. *(Encouraging.)* But you'll go back —

HEATHER. What do you mean?

MIRANDA. Well, you're young, you have time —

HEATHER. *(Brokenhearted.)* But I'm graduating. After that there is no more tall flag.

MIRANDA. Oh. I'm sorry … *(Beat.)* What is tall flag?

HEATHER. Twirling. Like with a baton? Only it's a flag. Didn't you have it?

MIRANDA. *(Tries to remember.)* No … I don't think so … *(Heather looks at Miranda like she's from another planet.)*

NICK. *(To Heather.)* Well, we had tall flag. In fact, my sister was a twirler. Let's order. *(A dorky waiter arrives.)*

WAITER. What can I get you?

HEATHER. *(To Nick.)* Can I have anything I want?

NICK. Anything at all.

HEATHER. I'll have a chocolate shake, fries, and a patty melt.

NICK. I'll have the same. *(He elbows Miranda.)*

MIRANDA. You know what? Me too. *(Beat.)* But no meat or cheese on mine. And I'll have tomatoes instead of potatoes. And a Perrier.

WAITER. Uh, we don't have Perrier.

MIRANDA. Pellegrino's fine. *(Heather looks at her curiously.)*

WAITER. Ma'am, this is a Denny's.

MIRANDA. Water.

NICK. So, Heather, is there anything you'd like to ask us?

HEATHER. Uh-huh. I made like a list —

NICK. Shoot.

HEATHER. What would you do if the child stayed out all night?

NICK. At what age are we talking about here?

HEATHER. Uhm ... seventeen?

NICK. Well, first I'd sit down and talk to her. I'd tell her I loved her and I was concerned.

MIRANDA. Right.

HEATHER. Would you smack her?

MIRANDA. We don't believe in corporal punishment.

HEATHER. What about hitting?

MIRANDA. Absolutely not.

HEATHER. *(Writes their answer.)* Okay. *(Reads.)* What if she wanted to stay over at a friend's and you knew there was going to be a boy there?

MIRANDA. You mean a boy boy? Or just a boy?

HEATHER. *(Defensive.)* Just a friend!

NICK. Gee, I don't think it would be such a good idea.

MIRANDA. Of course it depends on the situation — *(Heather looks back and forth between them.)*

NICK. Not really.

MIRANDA. What if a parent were home?

NICK. We're talking about a seventeen-year-old girl!

HEATHER. So is that like a yes or a no?

NICK. *(To audience.)* By the time pie came, we'd told her that yes of course we believed in God — *(A glance at Miranda.)* depending on how you defined God ... No, we didn't think a child should watch a lot of TV — *(A glance at Miranda.)* though some TV — and not just PBS and Bravo — was all right ... And we definitely thought a child could have a cat if they weren't allergic.

MIRANDA. *(To Heather.)* Or fish. Fish are good because they don't shed.

HEATHER. Well, thanks for lunch.

NICK. It was really wonderful to meet you.

HEATHER. *(Gets up.)* Uh-huh. *(He shakes her hand. Miranda starts to shake her hand too. Then she can't let it go.)*

MIRANDA. *(Emotional.)* Listen, Heather … . I just want to say … I think it's great that you're working to earn money for the prom … But — do you think — I mean would it be all right if … Could we give you the money for the dress?

HEATHER. *(Tears up.)* You want to like buy me the dress?

MIRANDA. *(Tears up.)* If that would be all right —

HEATHER. *(Moved.)* I guess … *(Nick takes out his wallet and hands her some bills. Miranda motions for him to give her more.)*

MIRANDA. Okay. Well, let us know what kind of dress you get. *(Heather nods and exits. The waiter removes the table, and Nick and Miranda are at Lila's.)*

NICK. *(To audience.)* We went home and waited for Judy to call. *(To Miranda.)* You know maybe we should do something to take our mind off this —

MIRANDA. Like what?

NICK. I don't know. We could make love …

MIRANDA. Nick — we're about to find out if we're going to be parents. I'm too excited to make love.

NICK. Okay … *(To audience.)* Judy called a few hours later.

MIRANDA. How'd we do?

NICK. We passed! *(They hug.)*

MIRANDA. *(Thrilled.)* We did?

NICK. She thought you were really neat!

MIRANDA. *(Beyond moved.)* She thought I was neat!? Did Judy get any information about the father?

NICK. He's eighteen, he's healthy —

MIRANDA. No drugs, violence, clinical or manic depression?

NICK. *(To audience.)* These were the things she'd decided were genetic — *(To Miranda.)* The only thing he put on the medical form was acne. *(Miranda beams. To audience.)* Heather and Miranda started to talk every other day.

MIRANDA. She had a sonogram! It's due in two weeks! Nick — it's a girl!

NICK. *(To audience.)* We bought a book called *What to Expect When You're Expecting.* *(A clerk brings it to Miranda who throws her arms around him.)*

CLERK. *(Looks at her stomach; dubious.)* Congratulations.

NICK. *(To audience.)* Expect to go shopping. *(They walk around with the book, dazed, shopping.)*

MIRANDA. Crib … changing table … mobile … bassinet … *(Nick's sister enters — unpregnant — and rolls a bassinet at them.)*

PAT. Here, take mine. Fuck it.

NICK. Thanks, sis!

MIRANDA. Diapers, Q-tips … *(Reading; with horror.)* Syrup of ipecac in case of poisoning? *(Miranda wanders offstage to shop some more.)*

NICK. *(To audience.)* While she was out shopping, Judy called. *(Miranda reenters with shopping bags.)*

MIRANDA. *(Eager.)* What'd she say?

NICK. Well, you know Heather thinks you're really neat …

MIRANDA. I think she's really neat too!

NICK. *(After a beat.)* But she decided to go with another couple. Her friend Liz has an aunt and uncle who just came over from Bosnia … and they had a miscarriage. *(Miranda manages to nod.)* And Heather felt bad for them. And she thought it would be better, since she was blonde, and the birth father's blonde, and the baby will probably be blonde … if both adoptive parents were blonde. *(Runs his hand through his dark hair.)* I'm sorry … *(Miranda can't find words. He puts his arms around her.)* Judy says it happens this way sometimes and we just have to get back on the horse.

MIRANDA. I don't know if I can get back on the horse, Nick.

NICK. *(After a beat.)* Why don't we go lie down for a while …

MIRANDA. I don't think so. *(She breaks free of the embrace and takes her shopping bags and the bassinet offstage.)*

NICK. *(Hurt, covers.)* Well, have faith, baby. We will get chosen. *(Lisa, twenty-three, enters. Punk, pierced, and eight months pregnant. There is a light change … and Lisa, Nick, and Miranda are in the middle of a meeting in a Lower East Side cafe.)* So when is the baby due, Lisa?

LISA. *(Laughs; tough.)* Whoa — soon!

MIRANDA. What does the doctor say?

LISA. I don't have a doctor.

NICK. But the baby — you've got to have a doctor —

LISA. Yeah, well, I'm a musician, I don't have insurance —

MIRANDA. How about the baby's father? Can't he — ? *(Lisa looks around, paranoid.)*

LISA. Look. Chaz doesn't know I'm doing this —

MIRANDA. He doesn't approve?

LISA. I showed him your resume. He said he was going to kill us. Which is why I need the living expenses Judy talked about 'cause I don't want to be in Brooklyn when he gets out of jail.

NICK. Well, that's understandable. Maybe we — or whoever you choose to adopt the baby — could —

LISA. Oh, I already chose you guys —

NICK. *(Excited.)* You chose us? You really chose us? That's — that's great! Thank you, Lisa! Listen, we'll find you a doctor today, and give you a call!

LISA. Okay — but I don't have a phone —

NICK. No phone?

LISA. It's a hundred and seventy-two dollars —

NICK. Listen, maybe I should write you a check — *(Nick gets out his checkbook.)*

MIRANDA. *(To Lisa.)* But you're moving, right? *(To Nick.)* Maybe she should move first and then get the phone —

NICK. It's not that easy to find an apartment, remember?

LISA. Oh, I found one, but they need a rent deposit —

NICK. Of course — *(To Miranda.)* You have to have a rent deposit —

MIRANDA. *(Meaning them.)* Sure — everyone needs a rent deposit, Nick — *(Nick hands Lisa a check.)*

NICK. Okay, here's a thousand to get you started. And I better give you some cash — *(He empties his pockets.)*

LISA. Hey, thanks a lot. *(She gets up to go. They get up too. Lisa stops and turns to Miranda. Suddenly, she's fighting tears.)* By the way ... I think it's a girl.

MIRANDA. *(Moved now.)* It's a girl? How do you know?

LISA. *(In tremendous pain, despite herself.)* Oh, you just kinda know ... *(Lisa and Miranda look at each other a moment. Lisa smiles, but it costs her. She starts to leave.)*

NICK. So we'll talk in a couple of days!

LISA. Right. Hey, thanks for the beer! *(Lisa rushes off.)*

NICK. *(To audience.)* We never heard from her again. *(Pause. They sit, leaving some distance between them, and we're back at Lila's.)*

MIRANDA. Well, at least we didn't have dinner. *(Blaming him.)* And lunch was only twelve hundred dollars —

NICK. *(Blaming her.)* Which I have to believe she needed just a little more than the new tennis court we bought for Dr. John Wilde!

MIRANDA. Well, maybe it was for the best. Chaz sounded like a pretty violent person. After all, he did threaten to kill us —

NICK. Threatening to kill is not genetic.

MIRANDA. No, but it wouldn't have been exactly good for the kid if we were dead —

NICK. Look — I'm going for a walk.

MIRANDA. Wait a minute. Why do you get to just go for a walk like that?

NICK. Do you want to go for a walk?

MIRANDA. No, I don't.

NICK. *(To audience.)* So nobody went. *(He sits down. They just sit there.)*

MIRANDA. After all, you can't just get up and go for a walk when you've got kids — their legs are too short.

NICK. *(To audience.)* We sat around the house for three days. I tried to comfort her —

MIRANDA. You really think that sex just makes everything okay, don't you?

NICK. *(To audience.)* Yes I do. *(To her.)* Of course not.

MIRANDA. You know, sex doesn't create intimacy. You need to have intimacy for there to be sex —

NICK. Oh, shut up. *(To audience.)* I probably didn't say that. I probably just said it to myself and watered the plants. Because I didn't really want to know why she didn't feel "intimate" —

MIRANDA. *(In the present.)* We were in the middle of a fight! What did you expect? *(She gets up and starts to leave.)*

NICK. *(To audience.)* I expected her to leave again. *(Miranda stops.)* Which is why I agreed to see the marriage counselor recommended by Paula — *(To Miranda.)* who was divorced! *(Miranda gives him a dirty look, as Harvey comes on and sits. Harvey has been doing this job for too long.)*

HARVEY. So. *(Sighs, bored already.)* Tell me about the marriage …

NICK. *(Mutters.)* Oh, that's original …

MIRANDA. Well, before he — *(Stops herself.)* before we decided to become parents, it was fine.

NICK. I think it was more than "fine."

MIRANDA. That depends on how you define "fine."

HARVEY. *(About as dry as you can get.)* So, would you say that you two see the marriage differently?

NICK. Well sure! And isn't that the beauty of a marriage — that there's two different people with two different points of view? That she sees the cup half-empty and I see it half-full? And somewhere in the middle is —

MIRANDA. I'm sorry. I flunked physics. What is in the middle of half-empty and half-full?

NICK. Well —

MIRANDA. Wait. What are we talking about here? What's in the cup?

NICK. Wine?

MIRANDA. I don't drink wine.

NICK. All right, coffee. Whatever you like.

MIRANDA. No — not "whatever I like." Don't be nice! What's in the cup?

NICK. *(To audience.)* Didn't I say wine? *(To Miranda.)* But you don't drink wine — so I'll take coffee. All right? Whether you can have caffeine or not. Is that mean enough for you?

MIRANDA. Fine. But I don't think you see the cup "half-full." I think you get a half-empty cup — and you see a double fucking latte! But it's — it's froth, Nick. The stuff you think is filling the cup has no substance. It's like — blind faith, it's all — foam!

NICK. And you — aside from not knowing a latte from a cappuccino — you see a perfectly good cup of coffee —

MIRANDA. Half cup —

NICK. Excuse me, a whole half cup of coffee … but all you see is a few measly little drops! No. A few grinds. No. One lousy grind! *(There is a pause. Harvey takes off his glasses and rubs the bridge of his nose.)*

HARVEY. Well, I'm not a coffee drinker … But can I ask a question here?

NICK.   MIRANDA.
Sure —   Yeah.

(Harvey is weary of them and all their kind.)

HARVEY. *(Had it.)* Why don't you just get a divorce? *(Beat.)*

NICK. *(In the present.)* You didn't say anything.

MIRANDA. Well, I don't think he actually meant —

HARVEY. Why don't you get a divorce?

MIRANDA. Well, I don't think —

NICK. You don't think you wanted a divorce or you don't think that's what he said? Because for all I know, maybe you're still thinking —

MIRANDA. *(Carefully.)* I think he may have said something about —

HARVEY. Hoping a child would save the marriage …

NICK. Look, what did you actually say?

HARVEY. *(Rises.)* Well, that depends on who's telling the story … *(He leaves. Twenty-year-old Isabel breaks through the back wall. Purple hair. Lime green Victoria's Secret pantsuit. Child from hell.)*

ISABEL. I AM! I'm tellin' the story! It's my story! Mine!

MIRANDA and NICK. Isabel!?

ISABEL. That's right. Isabel! I-Z-Y-B-L-E. Isabel!

MIRANDA. *(To Nick.)* Oh God. Why can't she spell? Does she have a learning disability?

ISABEL. I heard that. My real mom was a speed freak and my real dad was a fifteenth-generation alcoholic, so what'd you expect — *(Like a curse word.)* Mom?

MIRANDA. This! *(Looks at her outfit.)* What are you wearing!?

ISABEL. It's a lime green Victoria's Secret pantsuit. But don't worry, I'm taking it off soon. 'Cause I'm goin' over to the park — to get knocked up! Like my real mom!

NICK. Don't talk to your mother like that! Shut up! I mean — *(Regroups.)* Time out. Go to your room.

ISABEL. I don't HAVE a room!

NICK. *(Like a pissy kid himself.)* Well, neither do I!

ISABEL. Yeah, but, I didn't ask to be born! And I sure as hell didn't ask to be adopted! And you know what?

NICK and MIRANDA. What?

ISABEL. I'm going to find my real parents now and leave you shattered and lonely. And you know what else?

NICK and MIRANDA. What?

ISABEL. I'M VOTING REPUBLICAN! *(The phone rings. The three of them freeze. Ring. Ring. Then —)*

JUDY'S VOICE ON MACHINE. Kids, it's Judy! I just met a wonderful birth mom! Call me! *(Nick and Miranda look at each other.)*

ISABEL. What are you waiting for? Make the call. *(She exits. Pause.)*

NICK. Miranda? *(Pause.)*

MIRANDA. *(Softly.)* All right, Nick. One last time. *(A bunch of kids' toys are thrown onstage. We hear a little bit of a children's show in Spanish from a TV in another room. Lupe Santiago enters, and we are in her apartment in East Harlem. There's a soberness to this meeting.)*

LUPE. Hi, I'm Lupe, come in. *(She picks up toys, straightening up.)* Sorry I couldn't meet you at the Burger King like we said. One of my kids fell down 'cause the stairs was broke again, and I had to take him over to Mt. Sinai to make sure he was okay. Why don't you sit down?

MIRANDA. Thank you. *(They all sit.)*

NICK. How many kids do you have, Lupe?

LUPE. You mean with me? *(They nod, surprised at the question.)* Two. And I got another one with my mother in Puerto Rico. Look — I'm just gonna tell you like it is because the first couple I picked, after we had lunch and all, they changed their mind. *(Pained.)* And

I could be having this baby any day now, so ...

NICK. That's not going to happen here, Lupe. We want this child.

(Miranda nods. Lupe nods.)

LUPE. *(Presses on.)* So I already filled out the medical forms ... I don't take no drugs, and one of my kids was taken away for a little while, and it's on my record, but I'm just gonna tell you straight out, it was his father called the child welfare on me because he wanted Michael to go live with his parents.

NICK. How do your kids feel about the adoption?

LUPE. Oh, they don't know. They inside watching the TV. I don't let them out of the apartment unless I'm with them, because there's some bad people around here. *(Pause; with difficulty.)* I haven't told them I can't keep the baby. They're real sensitive kids, and their feelings get broke easy. *(Nick and Miranda nod.)* You're Christian, right?

NICK. Catholic. *(Miranda starts to say something — but doesn't.)*

LUPE. Yeah, me too. Only now I go to this other church with the Pentecostals, and they tell me it's a sin to give up my baby, and if I take Jesus into my heart, the baby will be okay. I told them I already have Jesus in my heart, and could they lend me the money for diapers and formula, and they told me to pray — *(Sounds of kids yelling. Lupe goes to a "door.")* Put it down, Michael! Don't be throwing things at your sister. Oye, the TV is not a toy. *(To Nick and Miranda; smiles.)* He's a good boy. *(To Miranda.)* So you can't have kids, huh?

MIRANDA. No. I — we ... No.

LUPE. I'm sorry. Kids are the greatest thing in the world.

MIRANDA. Yes?

LUPE. Oh yeah. They see you crying, they go, "Mommy, don't cry, we love you" ... *(Miranda smiles. Nick watches, heartened, as Miranda and Lupe start to connect.)* Look — I just want to do what's right, you know? I heard about this program at City College where you could become a court reporter, and I really like the court shows, you know?

MIRANDA. Yeah, me too.

LUPE. So I asked my worker and she said I could get childcare if I go back to school and get my GED — but how I'm going to do all that with another baby? But the people from the church say it's a sin — *(Yells to her son.)* No, you are not throwing nothing out no window! Oye, what's the matter with you? How you gonna throw a TV out the window with all them bars? *(To Miranda.)* He don't like TV. Four years old, he thinks he's a man. He sees his father leave, he goes, "Don't worry, Mommy. I'm the man." *(Laughs.)* Ay, dios mio — *(Miranda smiles. Then —)*

53

MIRANDA. Could we meet his father?

LUPE. What for?

MIRANDA. Well, the baby …

LUPE. It ain't the baby's father.

MIRANDA. Could we meet the baby's father?

LUPE. What for?

MIRANDA. Well, he's the father … Someday this child will have questions —

NICK. But we don't have to meet him if it makes you uncomfortable —

MIRANDA. But we'd like to meet him, if that's possible — *(Nick gives Miranda a look.)*

LUPE. *(Shrugs.)* Meet him. I put down his address on the forms. Oh listen — one thing I got to tell you because I might forget at the hospital. All my kids are allergic to milk. *(To Miranda.)* You better write this down. *(Nick and Miranda look for pens. Finally —)*

MIRANDA. *(To Lupe.)* Do you have a pen? *(Lupe gets her a crayon from the basket of toys on the floor.)*

LUPE. You need paper? *(They nod. Lupe gives her some drawing paper from a child's pad. Miranda starts to write. Nick gives her a children's book to put under the paper. They look like kids.)* So you got to use the soy formula.

MIRANDA. *(Writes.)* Soy …

LUPE. And two of my kids got bronchitis, so when they start coughing, you got to give the antibiotic right away.

MIRANDA. Penicillin?

LUPE. That's okay. *(Pats stomach.)* This one's pretty active, moves around a lot … But don't let the doctor give you none of them hyperactive drugs. They see a Puerto Rican kid that's active, right away they want to put her on the Ritalin. *(Upset, despite herself.)* They don't need that shit — they're just kids, okay?

MIRANDA. Okay …

LUPE. *(Emotional.)* You give them a lot of love, they'll be fine, okay?

NICK. Okay. *(Everyone is getting emotional now …)*

MIRANDA. But — we'll see you again before the baby's born, won't we, Lupe?

LUPE. *(This is getting very hard.)* Look, no offense, I like you all right, but … I think it's better if maybe you just come to the hospital, after …

MIRANDA. Oh …

NICK. But if you need anything — *(Nick starts to take out his*

wallet. Lupe gets up.)
LUPE. *(Fiercely proud.)* No. I don't. I don't want money for this. I don't want nothing. You just … *(Starts to cry.)* You just love her, okay? That's all. You just let her know that I loved her and — and this wasn't about her, okay? I want her to have a room that's hers! I want her to go outside! *(Fighting the tears.)* And you let her know about Jesus. You let her know that … she'll be fine. *(Nick and Miranda rise. Lupe holds out her hand to Nick, and they shake hands.)*
MIRANDA. Lupe — ?
LUPE. Yeah?
MIRANDA. *(Softly.)* How do you know it's a girl? *(Lupe puts Miranda's hand on her stomach.)*
LUPE. *(Smiles.)* Ay, m'hija. You just know. *(Miranda looks at her a moment and nods. Lupe picks up the basket of toys and leaves.)*
NICK. Miranda? I want this child.
MIRANDA. *(Sure.)* Yes. *(They embrace. Miranda exits.)*
NICK. *(To audience.)* We met Carlos, the baby's father, at the Burger King. He wasn't crazy about the idea of the baby going to people who were white, but he just couldn't afford to raise it right now. He was going to City College to be a drug and alcohol counselor … *(Miranda enters with two beers. To audience.)* He'd had a heroin habit himself, but he'd been clean for almost a year. *(Bit tightly.)* But Miranda was still a little concerned —
MIRANDA. *(Feels guilty for her concern, but …)* About possible chromosome damage to the baby — *(Miranda drinks her beer.)*
NICK. *(To audience.)* My sister had done a little heroin when she was a teenager, and her three kids were fine, so I didn't think we needed to worry —
MIRANDA. And there's the possibility of learning disabilities —
NICK. *(Tightly.)* Uh-huh … *(Continuing to audience.)* It seemed to me the parents were … good people.
MIRANDA. *(Surprised; wonders.)* You think goodness is hereditary?
NICK. Why would it be just the bad stuff?
MIRANDA. *(Thoughtful.)* I don't know. I just — I just always assumed we'd have a healthy child —
NICK. What about a healthy child with learning disabilities? Or a healthy child with Down's Syndrome? Or a child who's perfectly healthy — and even happy — who'll never subscribe to the *New Yorker*? How about just — a happy child?
MIRANDA. *(Thrown.)* I — don't know — where that comes from —

NICK. Well, is the happy part up to us? Or should we look for people who have happy genes?

MIRANDA. Of course not. Just as long —

NICK. *(Overlaps; to audience.)* As long as the parents were drug-free, or relatively drug-free, marijuana was okay — and as long as there was no history of violence … Though gangs didn't trouble her because you joined a gang for socioeconomic reasons, not genetic ones, so gang involvement couldn't be passed down. I don't know how she knew this having never been in a gang —

MIRANDA. *(Tipsy from beer.)* I'm not a joiner! *(She puts down her empty bottle and reaches for the one he hasn't started.)*

NICK. *(To audience.)* And as long as there was no alcoholism, because we know that's hereditary — even if you drink nothing but Perrier for your first thirty-eight years … *(Miranda puts down the beer. To audience.)* And as long as there was no history of clinical, as opposed to regular — *(To and re: Miranda.)* day to day, relentless, "normal" depression —

MIRANDA. I think you've made your —

NICK. *(Overlaps, to audience.)* And, of course, neither birth parent could have manic depression — 'cause if they did, then for sure, despite the wonderful environment we'd give the kid once we actually got an apartment … despite whatever wisdom we'd gained from more or less surviving our own childhoods … if one little manic-depressive gene snuck in there — *(Pause.)* Our kid would wind up … dead. *(Pause.)* Like her father.

MIRANDA. You have to do this in front of — ?

NICK. *(Goes to her.)* For Chrissakes, what about love, Miranda? Day to day, chronic, relentless … love!?

MIRANDA. *(Rises.)* I think you've made your point.

NICK. No. Here's my point. You know what all this worrying is?

MIRANDA. What?

NICK. BIRTH CONTROL! *(To audience.)* I don't believe I said that —

MIRANDA. *(In the present.)* And you also said —

NICK. Can we only love what looks like us — or eats like us — or prays like us? 'Cause then to hell with overpopulation — and the crap they put in school lunches — if that's the kind of marriage this is, maybe we shouldn't bring a kid into it at all!

MIRANDA. *(Stunned, wounded.)* I'm going for a walk.

NICK. Go. *(She starts to leave, turns.)*

MIRANDA. *(Evenly.)* Nick? I never said I wouldn't adopt that

child. *(They hold each other's eyes for a moment. Then she leaves.)*
NICK. Lupe kept her child. *(Pause.)* The Pentecostals went up to Carlos's apartment and convinced him that what Lupe was doing was a sin, and Carlos convinced Lupe ... and she kept the child. And maybe that was a terrible decision. And maybe it wasn't! We don't know. *(Fights tears.)* All we know is ... It wasn't our child. *(Pause; starts to leave.)* I have an appointment with a couple who want a mural. Deep blue sky, stars, maybe a couple of nice constellations ... *(Leaving; bitter.)* What kind of world do they think this is? *(He leaves. Sound of birds. Light change, dreamy. Women with baby carriages stroll through the park. Miranda enters and is surrounded by them. Slowly, they drift off, but one remains. Miranda peeks in the carriage.)*
MIRANDA. Cute baby ... *(The young woman is turned towards her child.)*
TINA. Oh — hey, thanks! *(Turns; realizes.)* Miranda!?
MIRANDA. Tina! Wow! You did it!
TINA. Yeah! I told this neighbor I wanted to adopt, and she knew this girl who couldn't keep her baby on account of she was on crack? And this girl came by our apartment — and the next week we had Faith!
MIRANDA. Well, I guess you have to —
TINA. No, Faith — that's her. *(Miranda looks at the beautiful baby.)*
MIRANDA. Faith is ... a crack baby?
TINA. Oh, she's not a crack baby! Her mom took the drugs. Want to hold her?
MIRANDA. Sure — *(Tina puts Faith in Miranda's arms. Miranda adores her.)* Hi ... Hi, little girl ...
TINA. See, I have this theory that all the souls waiting to be born know exactly where they need to go. Like maybe a child's born to a really poor family 'cause he's supposed to grow up and design really good low-income housing — with big windows — 'cause most projects are designed by people who never looked out of them from the inside.
MIRANDA. So you think the soul picks its parents?
TINA. And sometimes a soul is trying to get to you — but the only way it can get there is through some other woman's body.
MIRANDA. What — like smuggling?
TINA. See, there's all these souls out there — thousands and thousands just waiting! I mean — life is so precious, it's so beautiful, it's like ... Hawaii! You just want to get there any way you can.
MIRANDA. I see ...

TINA. Well, it's nap time.

MIRANDA. Oh, I'll be glad to watch the baby for you —

TINA. No — it's *her* nap time. Oh. You want — ? *(Tina nods.)*

MIRANDA. *(Heartbroken.)* Oh. All right ... *(Reluctantly, Miranda gives the baby back. Fighting tears.)* Bye-bye ... Bye, Faith. Bye, little girl ... *(She gets up. Tina hugs her.)*

TINA. Miranda? I just know — when it happens for you? You'll see that everything you went through was just part of the path.

MIRANDA. How do you know that, Tina?

TINA. *(Smiles.)* Oh ... you just know. *(Tina floats off.)*

MIRANDA. *(Calls after her.)* Wait a minute! Tina? What do you mean, "You just know"? What is that? Some sort of — "mom code"? *(Mutters.)* "You just know." I've never "just known" anything in my whole life! *(She realizes she's alone, talking to herself. Calls offstage.)* Nick — ? Nick, I'm all alone out here! *(She waits. Nothing. Finally ... To audience.)* I began to wonder if maybe I wasn't supposed to have a child. *(Pause.)* That all this trouble we'd been having was a sign. But from whom? I didn't believe in God enough to accept a sign from him. And I couldn't accept Nick's point about God playing dice with the universe, because I just didn't see God as a gambler. *(Pause.)* I thought He was a manic-depressive. Unpredictable, excessive, and yes, like my father, when you need him most ... dead. *(Calls offstage; softly.)* Nick? *(She waits a moment, then starts to exit. He enters and they walk right by each other. Nick has a bucket of paint and a brush. He starts to paint the fourth wall.)*

NICK. Judy didn't call. She said things were "slow." I got a gig painting multicultural angels on the ceiling of an Upper East Side preschool, and Miranda got a job coming up with those little slogans you see on mugs. *(Pause.)* Lila got her a book called *Childfree*. *(He paints.)* We got an apartment. Clean white walls. *(After a moment, Miranda enters. There's a politeness between them, a trying to make the best of it.)* How was work?

MIRANDA. Not too bad. I came up with a new one — *(She takes a mug from her bag which says ...)* "Hey, Some People Don't Even Have This Lousy Mug." *(He gives a thumbs-up.)*

NICK. You want dinner?

MIRANDA. I'm not really that hungry.

NICK. How about a sandwich?

MIRANDA. All right. *(They turn a moving carton into a dining table.)* I'll help you —

NICK. You don't have to.

MIRANDA. It's okay —

NICK. All right. (*They start to prepare for dinner. Plates, bread, olive oil. The awful politeness between them.*)

MIRANDA. Did you see the news?

NICK. No. Why, what happened?

MIRANDA. I don't know. I didn't see it. I thought maybe you —

NICK. Want me to turn it on?

MIRANDA. Not really. Unless you want to —

NICK. How about the radio?

MIRANDA. All right. (*He turns it on. Fauré's* Requiem *plays. Gorgeous. Heavy. Sad.*)

NICK. Turkey with tomato and onion?

MIRANDA. Please.

NICK. You want cheese?

MIRANDA. (*Pleasant.*) Whatever — (*They make sandwiches in silence. Then their hands touch — as both reach for the olive oil. It's the first touch in a while.*)

NICK. Sorry. You take it —

MIRANDA. No, no, you were about to — (*Nick starts to cry. She puts her hand over his. He kisses her hand. Holds on.*)

NICK. Is it a happy ending, Miranda? (*She kisses his hand, his face ... *)

MIRANDA. Happy enough. (*He nods. They start to eat their sandwiches. Then the phone rings.*)

NICK. Let it. (*They keep eating. Ring. Ring. The machine picks up.*)

JUDY'S VOICE ON PHONE. Nick? Miranda? It's Judy! Listen kids, a baby has just been born ... (*They keep eating.*) I'm at the hospital, and the baby seems fine. The birth mom's still here, and I'm trying to get some information — I know that's important to you, Miranda — but I don't think we're going to be able to get a whole lot. Let's see, I'm looking at my notes ... Okay. She's twenty-seven ... biracial ... didn't give any info about the father ... She may have done some drugs during the pregnancy ... And she doesn't want to meet the adoptive parents — but I need to know if you're interested right away because I've got other resumes with me, and she's going to be ready to leave the hospital in about an hour! So, call my pager number as soon as you get this! (*Pause.*) Oh — I almost forgot, kids — it's a boy! (*Click. Silence. They keep eating ... Then — both rise at once.*)

NICK.	MIRANDA.
I want him —	Let's take him —

NICK. You sure?

MIRANDA. Yes.

NICK. How do you — ?

MIRANDA. I just know. *(To audience; amazed.)* So sue me …
(Touches her heart.) You just do. *(The actor who played the clerk from
the bookstore comes on in scrubs and puts a baby in Miranda's arms.
Then he shakes his head and leaves. Sheer wonder.)* Nick — ? *(Nick
is looking at the baby. Beaming.)*

NICK. *(To audience.)* I swear on St. Jude, that's how it happened!
(To Miranda.) He's so beautiful!

MIRANDA. Nick, we're … parents! *(They look at the baby. At each
other. Then Miranda looks out at the audience — wonder and fear
and utter incredulity.)* Oh my God … *(The lights fade.)*

End of Play

PROPERTY LIST

Table with Thanksgiving dinner, chairs
Chairs
Desk with chart and chairs
Bed
Business cards, pens
Restaurant table and chairs
Baby carriages
Two chairs, newspaper (NICK)
Sandwich fixings, plates (NICK, YOLANDA, DOMINIC)
Books (MIRANDA)
Cigar (NICK)
Cigarettes, lighter (PAT)
Martini (LILA)
Carving knife (YOLANDA)
Bucket and mop (NURSE)
Sterile cups (NURSE, MIRANDA)
Shopping cart, doll (MOM)
Purse with newspaper (MIRANDA)
Business cards (RICHARD, GARY)
Prescription pad, pen (JOHN)
Books (CLERK)
Fake snow (MIRANDA)
Chairs with beaded seat cover (CABBIE)
Newspaper (CABBIE)
Money, purse (MIRANDA)
Martini glasses and pitcher (LILA)
Knife and sandwich on a plate (NICK)
Card (BOSS)
Sculpture (NICK)
Silver metal case (PAULA)
Tissues (MIRANDA)
Stuffed animals (MIRANDA)
Gurney (MIRANDA)
TV (SAL)
Grocery bag with juice and olives (MIRANDA)
Fingerprinting ink, paper (POLICEMAN)
Checkbook, pen (NICK)
Paper, pen (HEATHER)
Wallet, money (NICK)

Bassinet (PAT)
Shopping bags (MIRANDA)
Kids' toys (LUPE)
Crayon, paper, children's book (LUPE)
Two beers (MIRANDA)
Baby carriage with doll (TINA)
Bucket of paint, brush (NICK)
Purse with mug (MIRANDA)
Moving box, plates, bread, sandwich fixings, olive oil (NICK)
Radio (NICK)
Doll (MIRANDA)

SOUND EFFECTS

"Charge" fanfare
Ball game sounds, cheers
Phone ring
Children's TV show in Spanish
Birds
Fauré's *Requiem*

NEW PLAYS

★ **INTIMATE APPAREL by Lynn Nottage.** The moving and lyrical story of a turn-of-the-century black seamstress whose gifted hands and sewing machine are the tools she uses to fashion her dreams from the whole cloth of her life's experiences. "…Nottage's play has a delicacy and eloquence that seem absolutely right for the time she is depicting…" –*NY Daily News*. "…thoughtful, affecting…The play offers poignant commentary on an era when the cut and color of one's dress—and of course, skin—determined whom one could and could not marry, sleep with, even talk to in public." –*Variety*. [2M, 4W] ISBN: 0-8222-2009-1

★ **BROOKLYN BOY by Donald Margulies.** A witty and insightful look at what happens to a writer when his novel hits the bestseller list. "The characters are beautifully drawn, the dialogue sparkles…" –*nytheatre.com*. "Few playwrights have the mastery to smartly investigate so much through a laugh-out-loud comedy that combines the vintage subject matter of successful writer-returning-to-ethnic-roots with the familiar mid-life crisis." –*Show Business Weekly*. [4M, 3W] ISBN: 0-8222-2074-1

★ **CROWNS by Regina Taylor.** Hats become a springboard for an exploration of black history and identity in this celebratory musical play. "Taylor pulls off a Hat Trick: She scores thrice, turning CROWNS into an artful amalgamation of oral history, fashion show, and musical theater…" –*TheatreMania.com*. "…wholly theatrical…Ms. Taylor has created a show that seems to arise out of spontaneous combustion, as if a bevy of department-store customers simultaneously decided to stage a revival meeting in the changing room." –*NY Times*. [1M, 6W (2 musicians)] ISBN: 0-8222-1963-8

★ **EXITS AND ENTRANCES by Athol Fugard.** The story of a relationship between a young playwright on the threshold of his career and an aging actor who has reached the end of his. "[Fugard] can say more with a single line than most playwrights convey in an entire script…Paraphrasing the title, it's safe to say this drama, making its memorable entrance into our consciousness, is unlikely to exit as long as a theater exists for exceptional work." –*Variety*. "A thought-provoking, elegant and engrossing new play…" –*Hollywood Reporter*. [2M] ISBN: 0-8222-2041-5

★ **BUG by Tracy Letts.** A thriller featuring a pair of star-crossed lovers in an Oklahoma City motel facing a bug invasion, paranoia, conspiracy theories and twisted psychological motives. "…obscenely exciting…top-flight craftsmanship. Buckle up and brace yourself…" –*NY Times*. "…[a] thoroughly outrageous and thoroughly entertaining play…the possibility of enemies, real and imagined, to squash has never been more theatrical." –*A.P.* [3M, 2W] ISBN: 0-8222-2016-4

★ **THOM PAIN (BASED ON NOTHING) by Will Eno.** An ordinary man muses on childhood, yearning, disappointment and loss, as he draws the audience into his last-ditch plea for empathy and enlightenment. "It's one of those treasured nights in the theater—treasured nights anywhere, for that matter—that can leave you both breathless with exhilaration and…in a puddle of tears." –*NY Times*. "Eno's words…are familiar, but proffered in a way that is constantly contradictory to our expectations. Beckett is certainly among his literary ancestors." –*nytheatre.com*. [1M] ISBN: 0-8222-2076-8

★ **THE LONG CHRISTMAS RIDE HOME by Paula Vogel.** Past, present and future collide on a snowy Christmas Eve for a troubled family of five. "…[a] lovely and hauntingly original family drama…a work that breathes so much life into the theater." –*Time Out*. "…[a] delicate visual feast…" –*NY Times*. "…brutal and lovely…the overall effect is magical." –*NY Newsday*. [3M, 3W] ISBN: 0-8222-2003-2

DRAMATISTS PLAY SERVICE, INC.
440 Park Avenue South, New York, NY 10016 212-683-8960 Fax 212-213-1539
postmaster@dramatists.com www.dramatists.com